POLICY STUDIES IN EMPLOYMENT AND WELFARE NUMBER 2

*General Editors: Sar A. Levitan and Garth L. Mangum*

# Manpower Challenge of the 1970s: Institutions and Social Change

**Stanley H. Ruttenberg**
**assisted by**
**Jocelyn Gutchess**

The Johns Hopkins Press, Baltimore and London

This book was prepared under a grant from The Ford Foundation.

# Contents

# Preface

For four years, 1965–69, as Manpower Administrator and—for part of that time—Assistant Secretary for Manpower of the U.S. Department of Labor, I headed the new, fast growing, and sometimes turbulent federal organization concerned with employment and training.

In this capacity I was responsible for attacking the gap relating to employment between the disadvantaged who are not being served by the normal workings of the labor market and the manpower institutions of government which are supposed to assist them.

The history of the manpower programs of the sixties and the increased commitment to the disadvantaged is a chronicle of hectic activity, continuing experimentation, and remarkable achievement. We did not achieve all that we set out to do. I am hopeful, however, that these reflections will contribute to a clearer understanding of some of the problems we faced and will, thereby, permit us to move ahead in the future.

Certainly some of the problems lie in the organization of manpower programs: in the way they are planned, in the way money is distributed to achieve specific objectives, in the problems of sponsorship and of project operation, in conflicting and overlapping legislation, and finally in the way the federal bureaucracy itself is organized to carry out manpower policy. I intend to discuss in this essay how some of these organizational situations developed and how we moved to deal with them. That this story of the organization of manpower programs is also to a large extent the story of the evolution of a federal manpower policy of assistance to the disadvantaged and of a growing national commitment to the two goals of full employment and equal employment opportunity for all should not be surprising. In the achievement of national, social, and economic goals, and in the administration of programs to meet those goals, the administrator is constantly aware of the close relationship between substance and form, between policy development and operational realities. Putting the two together is the challenge faced by any administrator. I have set out here some of my experiences in trying to meet that challenge.

Although the experiences are mine, the preparation of this booklet could not have been accomplished without the helpful advice and assistance of many others. I am indebted to The Ford Foundation, under whose auspices this study was undertaken, and to the National Manpower Policy Task Force whose members provided initial guidance and continual support. My good friends and colleagues, Sar Levitan and Garth Mangum, deserve special appreciation for their painstaking and helpful review of the manuscript. The critical editing and diligent research work provided by Miss Barbara Weinstein have contributed immeasurably to whatever academic or literary value the booklet has. And, finally, to Mrs. June Jackson and Mrs. Gloria Scott, who have with unfailing good humor and unerring accuracy typed and retyped successive drafts, go not only my thanks but my heartfelt admiration.

**Manpower Challenge of the 1970s:
Institutions and Social Change**

# 1

## Introduction

> Man is the only creative animal on earth, though paradoxically his resistance to change sometimes can be heroically obstinate. He builds institutions in order to preserve past innovations, but in that very act often fails to promote the environment for growth of new ones. And so there are gaps that trouble our times.[1]

"Manpower" is a relatively new word in the lexicon of social and economic affairs. My concern with manpower is not with the traditional definitions relating to the physical strength of an individual or the collective availability for work of a group of people, but with a new meaning the word has assumed as a result of the government's growing interest in training the unemployed, the underemployed, and, especially, the disadvantaged. Government manpower policy has two basic goals: (1) to promote the full development of our human resources by assisting individuals—particularly the poor and the disadvantaged—in their adaptation to the world of work and in the fulfillment of their employment potential, and (2) to contribute to national economic stability and growth. It is the interaction of these two aims that defines the word "manpower" and that comprises the manpower policy discussed here.

During the period 1963 to 1969, when I was most closely associated with the government's manpower efforts, there was a concentration of energy on the social component of manpower policy —particularly on the development of manpower programs aimed at the disadvantaged. This emphasis can be ascribed to three major forces underlying domestic policy in the sixties.

First, the continuing existence of poverty in America became a major public issue. Under the leadership of Presidents Kennedy and Johnson a national effort was launched to close the gap between those who were caught in the self-perpetuating cycle of poverty and discrimination and the great majority of Americans who were enjoying the fruits of unparalled prosperity and growth. "It is therefore, the policy of the United States to eliminate the paradox of poverty in the midst of plenty in this Nation by opening to everyone the opportunity for education and training, the opportunity to work, and the opportunity to live in decency and dignity."[2]

Second, the civil rights movement erupted, and with it came a growing public awareness of the social, economic, and political deprivations incurred by minorities. Most significant was the recognition that discrimination is as destructive and wasteful of both human and national potential in employment as it is in education, or health care, or housing.

Finally, there was the threatening and increasingly complex urban crisis and the new federal-city relationship which developed to help meet that crisis.

As these forces of the sixties clashed with institutions created largely in the thirties, forties, and early fifties, it became clear that the institutions were not geared to respond to the demands for innovation or change. It is in this conflict that some of the major "gaps that trouble our times" are found.

In searching for the causes behind the development of the gaps, a significant but often ignored factor is the organizational structure itself—the intergovernmental system which must translate national policy into an identifiable event of change in an individual's life. The ability of this structure to perform is

2

measured, finally, by such little things as the correct referral of a young ghetto dropout to the most appropriate job or training opportunity; by the way local citizen planning groups relate to each other as they try to deal with the same sets of problems with different sets of resources; or by the exploitation of alternate avenues to federal authority and money by experienced local program operators.

These are the kinds of problems that are frustrating full effectiveness of our manpower programs today. Without some attention to such matters as coordination, delivery systems, and program integration, the elimination of poverty and the achievement of full employment remain phrases holding out promises that can never be realized.

It is time to bring together into a cohesive whole all of the parts of a national manpower policy, and it is time to devise an orderly system within which they can function.

It is not that innovation should be forgotten or put aside. If concern about manpower policy is to continue to be a dynamic part of the national domestic policy, there must always be innovation or change. But as things now stand, coordination can no longer be put off. Structural and organizational weaknesses of the manpower system leave little room for further expansion or extension of manpower policy. The case for coordination is not just a matter of economic prudence; it is even more a matter of thoughtful planning for a future in which the national manpower objectives of full employment and economic prosperity are met.

At the outset, I must stress that the attention this paper gives to the structural problems of manpower administration is not intended to detract from the substantive problems. Indeed, for the past eight years, the primary concern has been with the substantive aspect of manpower. The present accumulation of manpower legislation and program authority, developed during the sixties, is evidence enough of that concern.

In 1961 the federally sponsored manpower efforts consisted primarily of the federal–state employment service, an apprenticeship program, and a program to import low-cost farm labor in the harvest season, all under the Department of Labor; and the vocational education and vocational rehabilitation programs of the Department of Health, Education, and Welfare. In 1961 the cost of the federal manpower programs, including the farm labor program, was only $250 million. Today we have a far-reaching $3.5 billion manpower program that includes the broad range of training and work experience opportunities necessary to help individuals prepare for, find, and hold good jobs; an improved and enlarged employment service; and a program to move people off welfare and into productive employment, as well as a developing capacity to train people in the skills that the nation's advancing technology requires. While hardly any of the resources available to the Department of Labor in 1961 were deliberately aimed at helping the disadvantaged, today approximately 75 percent of the Department's programs are intended to help those least able to compete successfully in the regular labor market.

As the emphasis has shifted more and more toward helping the disadvantaged, manpower programs have grown in size and complexity. The ability of manpower institutions and organizations to adapt to the new demands of those programs has been severely tested. Much of the overlap, confusion, duplication, and disarray that exists today and is apparent in all elements of the present manpower organization is due to the uneven success of the existing manpower system in meeting this test of change.

## An Overview of Manpower Organization: Where it Stands Today

Any review of the present manpower organization must be concerned with four distinct areas: (1) the laws which set the stage for all manpower policy and programs; (2) the systems for planning and resource allocation; (3) the operational machinery or delivery systems; and (4) the federal administrative structure through which the public responsibility must be effectively and efficiently discharged.

The present body of manpower legislation has been developed

to meet the problems of specific groups of people who needed employment training and assistance, as their needs became known and identified. Starting with the Area Redevelopment Act and the Manpower Development and Training Act (MDTA), which were originally designed for the technologically unemployed, and moving through the incremental additions to the poverty program —the Neighborhood Youth Corps and the Job Corps for unemployed youth and school dropouts, the Title V Work Experience program for "unemployed fathers and other needy persons,"[3] Operation Mainstream and New Careers for the adult poor, and the Work Incentive Program for welfare recipients—the legislative authority for a comprehensive manpower program is now on the books. But the process of legislative development, involving as it does the interplay of political and social forces as well as personalities, individual ambition and goals, and special interests, has understandably resulted in a body of legislation that contains many inconsistencies and contradictory requirements. As a sample:

— The Manpower Development and Training Act requires some planning of manpower programs through a system of state and local advisory committees. The Economic Opportunity Act (EOA) requires planning through a Comprehensive Work and Training Program tied to a community action agency. Still another system, the Cooperative Area Manpower Planning System, exists by virtue of administrative action and Executive Order.

— Funding under the MDTA is to the states. Funding under the Work Incentive Program is through the Department of Health, Education, and Welfare to the Department of Labor, and then to the states.

— There is no clear distinction between client groups for the different programs. For example, there is no requirement in the law that enrollees in the Neighborhood Youth Corps out-of-school program be youths. The original upper age limit of twenty-one was removed in the last round of amendments; theoretically, anyone over sixteen can be enrolled in this program. The same group is also eligible for

JOBS. Or take welfare recipients. They are eligible for inclusion in most manpower programs, but there is also a special one just for them—the Work Incentive Program.

— Skill centers established by the Vocational Education system to provide occupational training to the disadvantaged must be given preference as a training resource in accordance with a requirement of MDTA. The Economic Opportunity Act insists on maximum feasible participation of the poor in operation and management as well as in planning and development of the poverty programs. Since Vocational Education is administered by states under their merit systems, the "poor" can hardly participate, and in fact do not assist in administration of the skill centers at all.

— Different programs have different systems of payment for trainees or enrollees. In most cases, the inequities have been corrected, but the fact that there is no one system for payment causes severe administrative problems.

— The legislative authority for the Employment Service is contained in the 36-year-old Wagner-Peyser Act, which mandates universal service to all comers and is, therefore, inconsistent with the requirements put on the Employment Service by the present spate of manpower legislation.

In addition to the contradictory requirements of the various laws—making it tough for a conscientious administrator to comply with congressional intent—the present system seriously undermines the principles of local planning and local control. The legislative framework of categorical programs, each divided into smaller and more rigid units as one moves from the national to the local level, in effect results in the imposition of a predetermined program mix on the local community. Until the inconsistencies and administrative flaws are removed, comprehensive and coordinated manpower planning and programming will not be achieved.

A coordinated, comprehensive program must be more than a glued together collection of separate pieces. It must be integrated, each piece with the other, so that the individual has available to him in an orderly sequence whatever he needs to move from unemployment and unemployability to a good job at a decent wage. It must provide a well-defined relationship to other social and economic development programs. Finally, it must provide a well-defined structure for carrying out a national manpower policy.

No clear pattern for manpower planning has been developed. In fact, the problem of providing a manpower planning mechanism has already been approached in three different ways: through the Cooperative Area Manpower Planning System (CAMPS); through the Comprehensive Work and Training Program system (CWTP); and most recently, through the Model Cities plan. None of these is totally responsive to either local need or national goals.

CAMPS is by far the most ambitious planning system, but it is essentially a state system for MDTA, with inadequate authority over the direct federal-local programs or other state manpower and supportive programs. Local CAMPS committees are intended to be area committees, one for each of the metropolitan areas.[1] But *area* planning, though it may make good economic sense, sacrifices political responsibility and cannot effectively substitute for *city* planning. In practice, local committees have not been able to function on an area basis. Overlapping jurisdictions, size and distance problems, and particularly the lack of political clout to make program and agency administrators get into line have generally frustrated the area planning concept.

The same problems are repeated at the state level. Although the governors have had the option of taking control of CAMPS, in general, until 1969, the chairman of the state committee has been one among equals, without authority over the rest of the members.* Furthermore, the state committee, without a statutory base or control over resources, has been forced to act in an advisory capacity—not as a planning body. State CAMPS committees have functioned more as assemblers of paper than as effective coordi-

---

* On June 6, 1969, Secretary of Labor George P. Shultz sent a letter to all governors urging them to "place greater reliance on elected heads of government" for planning. He offered grants to the governors for hiring planning staff of their own to supervise state manpower planning systems.

nators of programs and resources. The system seems to have put a premium on the "pile it up and pass it on" kind of planning, rather than on a careful assessment of needs balanced against available resources.

The greatest benefit of CAMPS has been its function as an information exchange, a means of interagency communication. The first step to coordination must be a shared knowledge of both programs and resources. CAMPS has succeeded in bringing this about and is appreciated by state and local officials for this reason.[5] But as a voluntary cooperative effort, without authority over program resources, real coordination of manpower programs remains a rarity, and coordination of manpower with other social and economic programs, a dream. Information sharing, however valuable, is not the whole of planning.

The second planning system imposed by federal fiat is the CWTP, authorized by the 1967 amendments to the Economic Opportunity Act. Still in the beginning stages of implementation, it is an attempt to make the manpower programs more responsive to local needs, but it is limited to manpower programs under Title I–B of the Act, with the notable exception of JOBS.

Under the Comprehensive Work and Training Program the local planning agent, presumably the local Community Action Agency, is a federally designated prime sponsor operating in a federally designated community planning area. Under present guidelines, designated community planning areas will tend to be whole metropolitan areas, not cities or counties. Under such a system there can be no provision for political accountability. Like CAMPS, the CWTP suffers from inadequate authority, incomplete program coverage, and unclear guidelines as to geographic parameters.

A third federally sponsored manpower planning mechanism just beginning to appear on the horizon is the Model Cities organization. In contrast to CAMPS and the CWTP, which exist solely for the purpose of promoting manpower planning, the Model Cities planning mechanism embraces all of the social and rehabilitative programs, of which manpower is only one part. However, the Model Cities system, while tied to the city government and involving the poor, completely ignores the states, and leaves unresolved the problem of how state controlled resources can be brought together in a city to achieve the Model Cities goals.

There is no consistent pattern of operations for manpower programs at the local level. It is not at all unusual to find several delivery systems within a single locality, each competing with the other for limited manpower resources, for clients within the target group, and for jobs or training slots to serve their clients. The development of the several systems is a direct result of federal legislative requirements plus expediency. MDTA put operational responsibility on the state agencies. The Economic Opportunity Act, however, with a direct contractual relationship between the federal government and the local sponsor, forced the development of another operational pattern, the selection of public and private nonprofit agencies as sponsors. The later imposition of the presumptive sponsorship of the EOA manpower programs by the Community Action Agencies (CAAs), and the development of the Concentrated Employment Program (CEP), brought another set of actors onto the stage. Now the requirement for City Development Agency sponsorship of the Model Cities program crowds the picture even more.

When I took over the Manpower Administration, it was a loose-knit confederation of three autonomous bureaus and a couple of staff offices, rather than a single administrative unit. With each bureau having its own field staff, often located in different cities and not in any regular communication with each other, independence was more in evidence than cooperation. Each bureau had its own line of communication to its field staff. In order to get even the simplest instruction to Manpower Administration field staff, it took at least three separate—and not always fully coordinated—sets of issuances. Even in the Washington headquarters, staff support services were provided in more than one place. Each bureau had its own supportive staff in addition to that provided directly to the Manpower Administrator. For example, on at least one occasion, at the same time that overall plans were being made for the total manpower program by Manpower Administration staff, plans for each of the separate programs were being developed in the bureaus—with no tie between the two.

The recent reorganization of the Manpower Administration as it appears on paper could go a long way toward correcting some of the defects that have stood in the way of a comprehensive program. But no reorganization, no shuffling of boxes and lines on an organization chart, can result in better administration without the right people to make it work. More significant, if the current Administration's thinking on the organization of manpower programs prevails—with its specific intent of moving manpower closer to a federal-state grant-in-aid system—the reorganization which was originally designed to strengthen federal direction and encourage local flexibility will have been an exercise in futility.

This quick sketch of the manpower system should provide some idea of the confusion, inefficiency, and complexity I have mentioned. A more detailed look at the forces which helped to shape the present organization—or lack of organization—will, I hope, suggest a possible solution.

# 2

## Manpower Legislation—
## Its Development and Operation

The legislative base for the programs administered by the Manpower Administration is made up of five separate pieces: the Wagner-Peyser Act of 1933, establishing the federal-state Employment Service system; the Fitzgerald Act of 1937, establishing a national apprenticeship policy; the Manpower Development and Training Act of 1962, providing occupational and skill training, manpower research, experimental and demonstration programs, and other related manpower services; the Economic Opportunity Act of 1964, providing employment and training opportunities for the poor; and the Social Security Act of 1935, with its amendments, authorizing the unemployment insurance system, providing the funding base for the Employment Service operations, and, as amended in 1967, authorizing a new program of work incentives for welfare recipients.

Manpower programs carried out by other agencies of government, and based on other laws—most notably the Vocational Education Act, the Vocational Rehabilitation Act, and the Demonstration Cities Act—though certainly important, are excluded from this discussion.

## Manpower Development and Training Act (MDTA)

The cornerstone of the present manpower legislative framework is the Manpower Development and Training Act of 1962. Amended in 1963, 1965, 1966, and 1968 to keep pace with the changing economic scene and shifting national priorities, the MDTA has proved to be one of the most useful and flexible laws ever written.

The initial thrust behind the legislation was the need to do something immediately for the large number of people already technologically unemployed (for example, the coal miners in Appalachia and the textile workers in New England), and the need to prepare for the increasing pace of automation which it was feared would soon displace additional thousands of workers in the auto, steel, electrical, and other industries. The MDTA marked the acceptance by the federal government of a social responsibility for the retraining of such technologically unemployed individuals so that they and their families would not be hurt by progressive economic developments that were producing benefits for society as a whole. Today the purposes which the MDTA fulfills are quite different.[1]

The threat of widespread technological unemployment did not materialize to any significant extent. Instead, it became increasingly evident that it was not the skilled workers, the family men with long-time work experience, who were being left behind. It was the disadvantaged who filled the ranks of the unemployed—those who were discriminated against or were never equipped in the first place to function successfully in the free labor market. The problem was the bottom of the labor barrel, not the top. In an expanding economy, skilled workers with education and experience easily adjusted to new work demands and occupational changes forced by technological advances. Faced with an increasingly tight labor market, industry managed easily to absorb whatever training was necessary to convert already skilled workers to new job requirements. But the unskilled, uneducated, inexperienced workers, including those denied experience because of discriminatory hiring practices, were very definitely being left behind. They were making up a larger and larger share of the unemployed.

As the overall unemployment rate went down from 6.7 percent in 1961 to 3.4 percent by early 1969, the gap between whites and nonwhites has remained fairly constant, the nonwhite rate staying approximately double that for whites. It is fair to assume that without the manpower programs this picture would have been worse. However, the gap between the disadvantaged and the rest of the labor force has widened insofar as teenagers are concerned. In 1961, teenage unemployment was two and one-half times the national rate. By 1968, it was triple the national rate. For nonwhite teenagers the picture is even grimmer; an increase from four times the national average in 1961 to seven times the average in 1968.[2]

When, as Economic Advisor to the Secretary of Labor, I first became involved in manpower programs in 1963, it was already evident that we were working on the wrong woodpile. It was also patently clear that the MDTA did not give us what we needed to cope with the really serious employment problems facing the nation, namely youth unemployment and the exclusion of the disadvantaged from effective competition in the labor market. The developments in manpower legislation over the next few years were directed almost entirely to these issues.

The Manpower Development and Training Act provides a classic example of effective institutional response to the need for social change. Far from being a static, self-perpetuating design dealing with the wrong problems at the wrong time, the MDTA, with its amendments, became a dynamic program meeting new and more pressing national problems as they arose. In theory our legislative process—involving the interaction of the executive branch, the legislature, and special interest groups—allows a continual adjustment of existing law to changing national conditions. But in the area of social and economic policy, existing legislation has frequently not kept pace with the need for change. Old laws and old programs die hard. Once they are established and a protective bureaucracy has been built around them, institutional arteries harden, resisting even the most obvious needs for change. This was not the case with the MDTA, however. The series of amendments over the first five years of the program followed a textbook pattern of operational experience, experimentation and evaluation leading to new legislative authority, and modifications and improvements in the program. A look at the chronology of these amendments will serve to demonstrate this evolutionary process.

As enacted in 1962, the MDTA was a relatively straight-forward, 100 percent federally financed program for classroom, or institutional, and on-the-job occupational and skill training for the unemployed. The funds are apportioned among the states on the basis of a formula. The Act also initiated a national program of manpower research. After one year it was to be a fifty-fifty matching program with the states.

*The 1963 Amendments* added a special program for unemployed youth, and authority for 20 weeks of basic education to prepare individuals for skill training. In addition, state matching requirements were postponed.

*The 1965 Amendments* added new authority for experimental and demonstration projects, job development, labor mobility projects, an experimental program to provide bonding for trainees, and special funds for training projects under the Area Redevelopment Act. It also liberalized allowance payments by increasing amounts for dependents and providing for transportation for trainees, eased the limitations on youth participation in MDTA, increased the permissible training period from 52 to 104 weeks, and set the matching requirement at 90 percent federal and 10 percent local funds for institutional or classroom training.

*The 1966 Amendments* added authority for a program for older workers, part-time training for low-skilled workers to upgrade skills in shortage occupations, physical exams and minor medical care for trainees, limited advance payments or loans to trainees, an experimental program for inmates of correctional institutions, and employability, or other-than-skill, training (i.e.,

14

prevocational instruction to introduce trainees to the world of work).

Other provisions were extension of the labor mobility and bonding programs; provision for the use of private training institutions in cases where the vocational school system could not do the job; relaxed eligibility requirements for participation in MDTA, reducing the labor force attachment requirement from two years to one and permitting youth to move from the Neighborhood Youth Corps into an MDTA training program; and revision of the apportionment process, reserving 20 percent of the funds for expenditure at administrative discretion, thereby providing greater flexibility for meeting national manpower needs.

*The 1968 Amendments* added new funding authority to encourage states to develop and administer comprehensive manpower programs. It revised the funding process by guaranteeing a minimum amount, $750,000, to each state, by permitting states to approve individual projects without further submission to federal authorities, when such projects had been included in a federally approved state plan, and by giving the states nine months, instead of six as before, to utilize the state allotment before it becomes subject to control by the federal government for reallotment to other states. Better utilization of existing skill centers was also required.

As can readily be seen, the amendments to the MDTA represent a continuing adaptation to new conditions and circumstances as they arose, dictated for the most part by the growing national concern with poverty and the employment problems of the disadvantaged, and the changing concept of government's role in meeting those problems.

The first set of amendments in 1963, adding basic education and a youth program, were the direct result of a better understanding of the problem of structural unemployment. Statistical surveys told us that the unemployed were disproportionately young and uneducated. Teenagers made up 20 percent of the unemployed but only 7 percent of the total labor force and only 7 percent of the MDTA trainee group.[3] Also, whereas 20 percent of the unemployed had completed less than eight years of schooling, only 3 percent of the first year MDTA trainees were drawn from this group.[4] The 1963 amendments were intended to help meet these problems.

When we learned that poor health prevented many trainees from getting the full benefit of the programs, we added provisions for health examinations and minor medical care. When it became apparent that existing programs were not getting at the special needs of older workers, a program for that group was initiated, though, unfortunately, that particular program has still not been as fully implemented as it should be. The addition of pilot programs to help workers move from depressed areas where there were no jobs to areas of high employment, to provide bonding insurance for individuals who could not qualify under the normal commercial standards, and to give pre-release job training to prisoners in correctional institutions were all added in an effort to spread the net of manpower training coverage to the groups who need help most—the "structurally" unemployed. Liberalization of training allowances and broadened eligibility standards further extended the ability of the MDTA to reach and help the disadvantaged unemployed.

Compared to other legislative programs for social and economic goals, the growth of MDTA has been accomplished quite painlessly. There has been acceptance of the need to shift purpose and scope to meet urgent national needs; in fact, manpower training legislation has enjoyed strong support from both sides of the aisle. The struggle has been over administration and implementation—a struggle that began with the first discussions in 1961 and 1962 and is still going on.

Once the need for manpower training legislation had been established, the overriding issue was whether responsibility for training and retraining adults should be part of the regular vocational education system or tied to the employment world. Since the vocational system was completely out of touch with the modern industrial world, it could not be trusted with such an assignment; moreover, bold new departures were necessary to meet new problems. Within the Labor Department there was strong support for government sponsored on-the-job training, which had proved so successful in meeting the World War II manpower requirements, particularly in training experienced workmen who found themselves with obsolete skills.[5]

Where classroom training was necessary, it was decided that it should be as closely integrated as possible with actual labor market requirements. The fear was that if the training program was given to the vocational education system it would end up as far removed from the real world of employment as the existing high school vocational education programs emphasizing home economics and agriculture. As late as 1964, 85 percent of high school students enrolled in a vocational education course were in home economics or agriculture. Only 12 percent were enrolled in trade or industrial courses. The Labor Department won the first round. The original administration version of the manpower training bill left the vocational education system out altogether.

The chief congressional supporters for manpower training legislation were Senator Joseph Clark and Representative Elmer Holland, both from Pennsylvania. Holland sided with the Department of Labor. Clark had his own bill modeled after a Pennsylvania state manpower training law which leaned heavily on vocational education. Furthermore, the vocational education system was not without other supporters. High on the list of effective Washington lobbies is the American Vocational Association, which went to work on the administration proposal.

The compromise reached in the end reflects the power of the vocational education system: the training program was divided into two parts—an on-the-job training program for which the Secretary of Labor would have sole responsibility and an institutional or classroom training program which would be jointly shared by the Secretary of HEW and the Secretary of Labor. Institutional training was to be carried out through the regular state-controlled vocational education system; but the decisions on occupations in which training would be offered and the selection of the trainees would be the responsibility of the Secretary of Labor. Regional review teams consisting of regional personnel from HEW

17

and the Department of Labor would have approval authority for individual training projects.

The case for giving the chief responsibility for the program to the Department of Labor rested not only on the argument that Labor was better equipped to handle the program but also in the belief that, in so doing, effective pressure could be brought to bear on the vocational education system to bring about much needed and far-reaching institutional changes. By giving the Department of Labor authority to determine what jobs people should be trained for, as well as the responsibility for the selection of the people to be trained, it was hoped that the vocational education system would be forced to shake off its outdated approach to the major employment problems facing the nation and would begin to make the adjustments that existing social and economic situations demanded. In fact, the theory is being borne out in practice. For example, a new division, separate from the old line Office for Vocational and Technical Education, was set up to administer HEW responsibilities under the Manpower Development and Training Act. It has served as a catalyst for change and has been able, to some extent, to force a shift of the resources of the vocational education system, making that system more responsive to present day employment problems, and particularly to the needs of the disadvantaged.

However, far from ending the struggle, the passage of the MDTA only marked the beginning. The vocational education system has continued its efforts to gain control of the manpower training program. The Labor Department, through its leadership, continued to resist—in part because the goal of providing employment assistance to the disadvantaged would be jeopardized, if not sacrificed, if control were entrusted to vocational education, and in part because of a conviction that only by developing and maintaining effective competition could institutions like vocational education be forced to change to meet new needs.

The early difficulties with MDTA institutional training were directly related to the inflexibility of the school systems. The schools where MDTA training was to take place were not near the areas where the would-be trainees lived. Classrooms were available at inconvenient times. Often they were unsuitable, having been designed for young people, not adults. Equipment and curriculum for training in the occupations certified by the Labor Department were not readily available. It was often difficult or impossible to hire qualified instructors for short-term training courses. The need for basic education, counseling, and job finding assistance, which must be closely related to the vocational instruction, could not be met when the individual trainee had to go to several different places around town in order to get these services.

The skill center, therefore, was jointly developed by the MDT division of HEW and the Manpower Administration of Labor as a new kind of vocational education plant to be administered by a school system. In concept, the skill center would provide in one place both basic or remedial education and training in a variety of skills geared to the needs of the local labor market. The center would be convenient to the neighborhoods where most of the target population live. In addition to skill training, the enrollees would also be able to get in the center the counseling and guidance they needed to make effective use of their training, as well as assistance in finding a job when they finished the course. The staff of the center would be hired specifically for the MDTA program and trained to deal with the disadvantaged. By the end of 1968 there were 55 skill centers in operation throughout the nation. About 20 percent of total MDTA institutional trainees are enrolled in these skill centers, which also absorb about 20 percent of the funds.

One of the chief issues in the development of the 1968 amendments was the utilization of the skill centers—really another facet of the vocational education fight for control. However this issue cannot be viewed as just one more Washington bureaucratic contest between two departments. It goes beyond that.

The argument in 1968 for vocational education control was multifaceted. It was an argument for the protection of a large government investment, for the utilization of professional expertise developed over a long period of time, and for the concept of vocational education as an integral part of the broader educational responsibility for the development of the whole man. But it was also an argument for state control of federal program dollars. In every state there is a Vocational Education Board which has long controlled the expenditure of federal vocational education funds. Generally these boards have not been responsive to the changing industrial patterns or, more particularly, to the changing education requirements of the cities.* My interest, and that of the Department of Labor, was not confined to the Washington power struggle.

Opposition to relinquishing control of the institutional program to HEW was based on an unwillingness to turn it over to a system controlled by these state vocational education boards. The opposition was not based on any disagreement with the concept of the skill centers, which were, after all, jointly developed by the Manpower Administration and Vocational Education. So long as the federal government through the Department of Labor retains authority to specify who should be trained and for which jobs, the program can be made responsive to the national needs. That is the key.

When the MDTA came up for renewal in 1968, the administration asked for a simple extension. By that time the MDTA had gone about as far as it could go. There was no need to liberalize it further as a separate piece of legislation; what was needed was a comprehensive manpower act incorporating the MDTA, and this was not the year for such a step. But the vocational education group saw this as an opportunity to strengthen its hold on the program— a hold which had been slipping each year as a larger and larger

* Given the historical distribution of vocational education dollars, it is highly unlikely that they will soon reach urban areas. Since passage of the *Vocational Education Act of 1963* (Public Law 88–210), the dollar distributions) have not coincided with the population distributions of the states. Twenty-nine percent of the disadvantaged population resides in the nation's 50 largest cities, but only 15 to 16 percent of vocational education funds flow to those cities. (Unpublished papers of the President's Task Force on Urban Education.)

proportion of the total MDTA appropriation went to on-the-job training instead of to institutional training.[6]

Two aspects of my administration of the manpower program presented ready-made targets for the campaign of the vocational education group in 1968: the transfer of MDTA funds to the new administration programs (the Concentrated Employment Program or CEP and Job Opportunities in the Business Sector or JOBS) and the reported underutilization of the skill centers.*

MDTA calls for an apportionment of funds among the states which then becomes the basis for state and local planning of manpower programs. But there was a provision in the Act for a redistribution of the apportionment by the Secretary of Labor after the first six months of the fiscal year. In practice this meant that funds, including institutional funds, that had not been obligated by January 1, could be redirected if the national interest required such a redirection and if proper notice were given to the states.

Manpower is a particularly dynamic field of government policy. Unlike many other kinds of social programs, the economic and social impact of the expenditure of manpower dollars is relatively quick and highly visible. This is one reason why manpower is so important as a tool of economic policy. It also means that manpower programs are especially suited to implementing shifts in national needs and priorities. The initiation of the CEP, con-

---

* Dr. Jack Michie, Director of the East Bay Skill Center in Oakland, California, stated that his center operated at about 50 percent capacity, "not because we don't have the funds to operate at full capacity but simply because the restrictions that are placed on us by a project type of funding, prohibits us from operating at full capacity." (U.S. Congress, House, Committee on Education and Labor, *Hearings on H.R. 15045, Manpower Development Training Act Amendments of 1968*, 90th Cong., 1st sess., 1968, p. 97.) Charts showing the enrollment fluctuations in the Oakland center as well as in the Miami, Philadelphia, Detroit, and Phoenix centers were presented, and Dr. Michie indicated that his conversations with the directors of these centers reflected a situation similar to his. Three skill centers—the John F. Kennedy Center for Vocational Education in Philadelphia, the Syracuse Skill Center, and the Fort Worth Skill Center—experimented with annual funding in FY 1969. While this method is admittedly better than the project type funding, it does not seem to have solved fully the problem of underutilization.

21

centrating manpower resources in a few selected cities and rural areas, and the JOBS program, offering new incentives to private industry in the fifty largest cities to hire and train the hardcore, both reflect the adaptability of manpower policy to such shifting priorities. Both programs were developed and instituted to fill immediate and pressing national needs, and therefore took priority over existing programs which, though desirable, were less suited to the immediate demands. In order to finance both the JOBS and the CEP, we used the authority which the Act gave the Secretary of Labor to reapportion unused MDTA funds after the end of the first six months of the fiscal year. In neither case did we take this step until we were assured that the most urgent needs of the states would be met. But the practical result was that a large band of state and local officials, including the vocational education people, felt that the Department of Labor had cheated them out of what was rightfully theirs. They did not find it hard to obtain agreement from congressmen and senators, especially those from states without either a CEP or a JOBS program.

In the case of the skill centers, HEW claimed that the Department of Labor was pursuing a deliberate policy of side-stepping the existing centers and ignoring their capability, with the result that a large federal investment in plant and equipment was being needlessly wasted. The problem became most acute with the Concentrated Employment Program. The concept of the CEP is that there should be made available to the individuals who live in a concentrated target area all of the manpower services that each individual needs in order to bring him from unemployability to permanent employment in a decent job. Skill training should, of course, be included in the range of services offered. It seemed reasonable to expect that the CEP enrollees should get the skill training they needed from skill centers where they were available. But in many instances a conflict arose between the skill center and the CEP, with the CEP insisting that the skill center should provide training without reimbursement, and the skill center refusing to enroll CEP enrollees without payment from the CEP. The real trouble was, of course, that there was never enough money to do the full job that needed doing. In any case, the argument that the skill centers were being underutilized was convincing enough to most congressman, and the law was amended to require that the centers be given first preference, not only for occupational training but for basic education and other employability training as well.

The 1968 amendments represent a departure from the established pattern of change in the MDTA. For the first time, the force behind the amendments was not the necessity of modifying the program to accommodate the emerging identification of the structural unemployment problem, but—as is more common in Washington—a power play of one group of interests against another. The adinistrative flexibility of the 1966 Act was curtailed, the interests of the states were strengthened, and the vocational education system won a firm foothold in the area of manpower training. Whether or not this will tend to undercut our efforts to concentrate the manpower effort on the disadvantaged remains to be seen.


## ECONOMIC OPPORTUNITY ACT (EOA)

In the early sixties the prevailing economic argument was whether the stubbornly high unemployment rate, ranging from 5½ to 6½ percent, was the result of insufficient aggregate demand or whether it was a purely structural problem. Was there unemployment because there was not enough demand fully to utilize the total labor force, or was it because there were people in the labor force whose lack of training and skills made them unfit for the available jobs? Were the shortcomings in the economy or in the people? Although we have since learned that the root causes of unemployment are in both, my concern at that time was that the structural problem would be overlooked by the "new" economists in their desire to prove their aggregate demand theories.

As early as 1963, Secretary Wirtz and I were having conversations with Charles Schultze, then Assistant Director of the Bureau of the Budget, on the question of government policy in regard to the structural problem. The Accelerated Public Works Act of 1962, directed mainly toward reducing structural unemployment in depressed areas, was due to expire, leaving a gap which we felt must be filled. We proposed a program of labor intensive public works employment. Schultze and the Council of Economic Advisors argued effectively against such a program, however, on the ground that the cost would be too high, and further, that in order to prove the aggregate theory, the anticipated tax cut of 1963 (which was finally passed in 1964) should be allowed to work its magic unimpeded by extraneous employment programs. But by 1964, when poverty became the principal domestic concern, the structural employment problem could no longer be pushed aside. At the same time that we in the Department of Labor were beginning the process of adapting the MDTA to meet the employment problems of the poor, the development of a strategy for a War on Poverty was well underway.

It seemed to us that employment was the key to the War on Poverty. But there was a difference of opinion among poverty planners, particularly in the Task Force established by President Johnson and chaired by Sargent Shriver which had the responsibility for the development of the administration's antipoverty legislative proposal. In the Task Force, the argument was whether the strategy should be based on a large-scale employment program or on community action, a newly developed concept in which the government subsidized the organization of the poor as a political and social force for self-improvement. Secretary Wirtz held that the "war" must begin with priority emphasis on employment if it were to have an impact on the poor, and that the program should be handled by the Department of Labor so that full advantage could be taken of the existing manpower machinery. Secretary Wirtz's personal representative on the Shriver Task Force was Daniel Patrick Moynihan, then Assistant Secretary of Labor for Policy Planning. He argued Wirtz's position, but evidently was eventually persuaded to agree with the rest of the Task Force that community action offered such a promising route out of poverty for ghetto residents and the isolated poor that it should be given top priority rather than employment. At a meeting at the Johnson ranch on the Pedernales, attended by Wirtz, Shriver, and Secretary John Gardner of HEW, the final decisions were made on the poverty plan. Wirtz made a last effort to include a large public employment program for adults, but it was rejected by the President as being too costly.

Although the administration bill that was sent to Congress included the chief elements of the twice stymied Youth Employment Bill of the Department of Labor, as well as a program of work and training for unemployed heads of households, primarily welfare recipients, it did not get at the employment problems of adults, nor at the needs of the large mass of the structurally unemployed.

In fact, many of those involved in development of the Economic Opportunity Act felt that the prime focus should be on youth, in the belief that the best (and perhaps the last) chance to break the cycle of poverty lay in providing jobs and other services for young people, before they were caught irrevocably in the downward spiral of poverty. The youth employment programs—the Job Corps and the Neighborhood Youth Corps—together with community programs aimed at improving the health, education, and rehabilitation of both children and youth were expected to be central components of antipoverty programs. (Headstart, which later became the mainstay of many local community action programs, was an afterthought—hastily designed in the spring of 1965 to sop up unused community action funds before the end of the fiscal year.) In the first year's appropriations, FY 1965, at least half of the total was allocated to programs specifically for children and youth.[7]

To build the broadest possible base of support for the Act in its entirety and to satisfy the competing demands of the several departments, the work-training and employment programs were split up among three federal agencies—a split that was agreed to at the Pedernales meeting. The Job Corps was kept by the Office of Economic Opportunity both because of its innovative character and because of its personal appeal to Sargent Shriver, who became the first director of the OEO. The Department of Labor got the Neighborhood Youth Corps. And the Department of Health, Education, and Welfare was given Title V, Adult Work Experience, a program primarily for welfare clients designed to supplement the lagging Community Work and Training program of the Social Security Administration. This dispersion of the anti-poverty manpower programs, plus the specific authorization of manpower as a program option for the new Community Action Agencies, formed the basis for much of the trouble with coordination in the months to come.

During its first three years, the War on Poverty lived a more or less transitory existence, dependent on both annual authorization and on appropriation from a critical Congress. The opportunity for continuous amendment to the EOA which the one year authorization provided has had both advantages and disadvantages. Although this process encouraged steady development, continuous adjustment, and even improvement in the poverty program, administrators were forced to operate with such uncertain authority that rational planning and consistent implementation were hard to achieve. However, on balance, I think that the constant amendment process was a good thing. It certainly allowed us to benefit from experience and to correct deficiencies in the original planning of the program. This was particularly true in the manpower area. Amendments to the EOA each year have gradually moved the total program more and more in the direction of employment and manpower as a strategy against poverty. Table 1 shows the relative distribution of the EOA resources for employment manpower programs as compared to resources for unearmarked community action programs.[8] Funds for the Title V program were omitted from the calculations since that program was replaced by the Work Incentive Program.

The first addition to the Economic Opportunity Act manpower package was a community improvement work and training program for chronically unemployed poor adults. Proposed by Senator Gaylord Nelson of Wisconsin, it passed without significant opposition in the fall of 1965. Like other manpower programs that

Table 1.  Comparison of economic opportunity act appropriations allotted for manpower and unearmarked community action programs.

|  | (in millions of dollars and percentages) | | | | |
|---|---|---|---|---|---|
|  | 1965 | 1966 | 1967 | 1968 | 1969 |
| Total OEO appropriation | | | | | |
|   dollars | 800 | 1500 | 1664 | 1753 | 1948 |
|   percent | 100 | 100 | 100 | 100 | 100 |
| Unearmarked CAP | | | | | |
|   dollars | 237 | 286 | 250 | 352 | 327 |
|   percent | 30 | 29 | 15 | 21 | 17 |
| Manpower programs | | | | | |
|   dollars | 315 | 592 | 633 | 764 | 922 |
|   percent | 39 | 39 | 40 | 44 | 47 |

SOURCE: OEO and the Department of Labor.

followed, this program (now known as Operation Mainstream) was designed to fill in part the gap left by the omission of a large adult employment program in the original Act.[9]

Conservation has always been one of Senator Nelson's major interests.[10] He saw this program as serving two important purposes: the conservation of natural resources and the provision of useful jobs for poor adults, particularly in rural areas such as northern Wisconsin where jobs were scarce. As it turned out, Operation Mainstream soon became more of a work program for older rural workers than a full-scale conservation program. As Secretary Wirtz commented, the program would more aptly have been named "backwater" than "mainstream."

Although Mainstream was definitely a manpower program, it was made part of Title II, the Community Action section of the Economic Opportunity Act, and as such it was administered directly by the Office of Economic Opportunity, not delegated to the Department of Labor. This was contrary to the purpose of the newly established Manpower Administration, and during the debate on the amendment, we made an attempt to get the Nelson program delegated to Labor. But the issue of manpower coordination was not considered crucial at that time; no strong objections were made by Senator Nelson; and Labor did not push the point when the OEO decided the program should be part of the CAP.

27

The 1966 amendments added two more manpower programs aimed at the adult unemployment problem. First was the New Careers program introduced by Congressman James Scheuer of New York as an amendment to Title II.[11] Scheuer had become interested in an experimental program, carried out by the Center for Youth and Community Studies at Howard University in Washington under an Experimental and Demonstration grant from the Department of Labor, in which some professional jobs in the social service fields were being "restructured" into their simpler and less technical components. The objective was to break down professional jobs so that the semiprofessional and subprofessional aspects of the jobs could be handled by individuals with less than full professional training. In the Howard University pilot project, hard-core unemployed from the ghetto area were being trained successfully for paraprofessional and subprofessional jobs in a variety of community service occupations.

Many manpower experts, both within the government and outside, were convinced that the program held promise; if extended on a national basis it could become a double-edged sword: helping to fill the urgent unmet demand for human services and, at the same time, providing useful employment for the hardcore—employment that could lead to rewarding careers. The House Committee on Education and Labor had already come to the conclusion that the primary thrust of the antipoverty effort should be on jobs, and a majority were easily persuaded that the New Careers program sponsored by Scheuer would be a valuable addition to antipoverty legislation.

The House Committee, however, suggested a merger of the Nelson and Scheuer programs so that there would be a single program of employment in the public sector, with maximum flexibility in local administration. In fact, the Committee Report specifically mentions the need to concentrate resources rather than spreading them across the nation according to formula.[12] But the Senate Committee, wanting to protect the special interests of the constituency that had already developed in support of the Nelson program, kept the two programs separate, and the separation was maintained in the bill as it was finally passed. Furthermore, the retention of both programs under Title II of the Economic Opportunity Act made them subject to a state allocation formula that further fractured and dissipated their impact.*

The second manpower program added to the Economic Opportunity Act in 1966 was the Special Impact program, or Title I-D. This program, developed jointly by Senators Jacob Javits and Robert Kennedy of New York, was conceived as a large-scale experiment involving private industry in the antipoverty effort and testing the theory of concentration of resources and the possible multiplier effect of such concentration. By attacking the multiple problems of a specific target area simultaneously, it was hoped that a real and noticeable change would occur in the lives of the area residents and that the advantages gained would spread outward and affect wider and wider areas. The purpose was to make a visible impact that would lead to successful and successive replication. Originally planned for $150 million, as it was finally adopted Title I-D was allocated $25 million—definitely an experimental program.

The addition of these two manpower programs to the Economic Opportunity Act in 1966 brought the total number of federal manpower programs aimed at the disadvantaged to seven: MDTA, Job Corps, Neighborhood Youth Corps, Title V Work Experience, Operation Mainstream, New Careers, and Special Impact. The case for coordination was self-evident. A policy decision was made to put the responsibility for administering all of the programs in one place—the Manpower Administration. However, implementation of that policy did not take place without a struggle.

---

* Under the Title II allocation formula, program dollars must be distributed among the fifty states, with every state getting its fair share of Title II money. The Title I distribution formula is much looser and does not require that each state get something. Originally, the only prohibition was that no more than 12½ percent of the money could be spent in any one state. Obviously, under this system it would be possible, if not politic, to overlook some states, a practice not favored by congressmen or by the comptroller general.

## The President's Committee on Manpower

During the spring and summer of 1966, at the same time that the second round of EOA amendments were being debated on the Hill, the administration undertook a major effort to improve the coordination among existing manpower programs. The story of that effort illustrates the point that the difficulties in coordination are not confined to state and local activities. In fact, local problems often only mirror the jealously guarded autonomy of Washington agencies and bureaus.

As early as 1964, the President issued an Executive Order establishing a President's Committee on Manpower (PCOM) to fulfill the requirement of Title I of the Manpower Development and Training Act that the Secretary of Labor advise the President and make recommendations on national manpower matters.[13] The PCOM consisted of the Secretary of Labor as chairman and the heads of the departments and agencies primarily concerned with manpower affair. During its first year the committee concentrated on the major problems of the day; that is, identifying manpower requirements and the need for training and retraining of scientists, engineers, and specialized personnel for new federal programs. But in 1965, when I became the Manpower Administrator, the committee turned its attention to what was fast becoming the paramount issue—the need for coordination of manpower efforts, particularly at the local level. Operating through a special task force, the PCOM decided to send federal representatives to each of thirty cities to explore their problems in detail and to act as catalysts for the integration of local manpower efforts.

It seemed only logical that the Department of Labor, as the chief manpower agency should send its representatives to the designated cities. However, neither HEW nor the OEO—both represented on the PCOM and both having a large stake in manpower matters—were ready to trust the Department of Labor with such an assignment. After several long and heated discussions a compromise was reached; it was agreed that there should be thirty three-man teams representing Labor, HEW, and the OEO, with the chairmanship of the teams divided among the agencies, each agency having its representative head ten of the teams.

By early spring 1966, the teams were operating in all 30 cities, reviewing local situations, and in some cases successfully bringing about improved coordination. However, without line authority or permanent assignment, their effectiveness was limited.

The major findings of the teams, which became part of the background for the congressional debate on the amendments to the Economic Opportunity Act, made crystal clear the urgent need for coordination.[14] In each major metropolitan area there were fifteen to thirty separate manpower programs administered by public and private agencies, all supported by federal funds. Prospective clients were badly confused, and serious gaps emerged when the programs, which should have been complementary, were developed separately.

Although it was generally accepted both in Congress and in the administration that coordination would be improved if the administration of manpower programs were lodged in one agency of the federal government, the concept of comprehensive manpower legislation had not jelled, even among manpower experts. The time was not ripe for such a major step. So, when the Economic Opportunity Act amendments became law in November 1966, they did not include provision for a single manpower agency. Responsibility for working out a means of coordination was left to the executive branch, where the issue emerged in the series of negotiations between the Department of Labor and OEO on the terms of delegation of authority for the operation of the new programs.

There was no disagreement between the top levels of the administration—Wirtz and myself in Labor, and Shriver and Bertrand Harding in the Office of Economic Opportunity—on the basic principles that should apply to the manpower programs under the Economic Opportunity Act. We agreed, first of all, that the programs should be brought together in one agency, and that since the Department of Labor was already administering the Neighborhood Youth Corps and the MDTA and would shortly become involved in the Title V Work Experience program, the

Nelson-Scheuer and Kennedy-Javits programs should also be delegated to Labor to be administered under the Manpower Administration. Second, all community based work and training projects under the Economic Opportunity Act should be closely related to the local community action agencies. And third, since the new programs touched directly on the spheres of interest of both Labor and the Office of Economic Opportunity, the guidelines and regulations should be developed jointly.

However, many people in OEO, particularly the Community Action Program staff, felt very strongly that the manpower programs should *not* be given to the Department of Labor. They feared that the result would be a turnover of the programs to the Employment Service where they would either languish and die or be diverted to the nonpoor. Even though a Human Resources Development program aimed at the disadvantaged had been initiated by the Employment Service, the credibility problem of this agency vis-à-vis the poor was still acute. It was argued that coordination was worthless if it meant assigning the poverty manpower programs to the Employment Service and what was believed to be certain death.

As a result of the pressure brought by the Community Action Program staff, as well as by minority organizations and other special interest groups, there was an agreement that the programs would not be administered by the Employment Service but would be brought together in a new bureau within the Manpower Administration. And to assure that the Employment Service would be kept at arm's length, Labor also agreed that first preference for sponsorship of the Economic Opportunity Act programs would be given to the Community Action Agencies.[15]

Even with these agreements, there were still some unconvinced OEO people who could not accept the transfer of programs and authority to the Labor Department without a struggle. As a result, the negotiations over details of guidelines and regulations dragged on throughout the winter. It was not until March 14, 1967, that the programs were officially delegated to the Manpower Administration—with only three-and-half months left of the fiscal year to get projects started and appropriated funds obligated. But already the wheels of the Washington legislative cycle were grinding, and we were caught up in the development of the next round of amendments to the Economic Opportunity Act, as well as with getting a new program started—the Concentrated Employment Program.

### Economic Opportunity Act Amendments of 1967

The manpower programs that were added to the Economic Opportunity Act in 1965 and 1966 were initiated by members of Congress. In 1967 the administration took the initiative. In his Manpower Message in April 1967, President Johnson had outlined the new directions that the national manpower effort should take. The three areas of concern that he stressed that year accurately reflected his substantial interest in and commitment to a national manpower policy.

The President highlighted:

—the necessity to focus our efforts so that we could get at the concentrated unemployment in the slums, which special Department of Labor surveys had shown to be about three times the average for the rest of the country;

—the need to involve fully the resources and expertise of private industry in the antipoverty effort, particularly in regard to problems of training and employment; and

—the need to make the overall manpower effort more efficient through better coordination and integration of the many new manpower programs.

The 1967 Economic Opportunity Act amendments, enacted just two days before Christmas, gave us the authority to move ahead in the directions outlined by the President.

Title I of the Act was completely revised to cover both youth and adults. The new name of the title was "Work Training and Work-Study Programs." It included the Job Corps as Part A (as before), and it broadened Part B—formerly the Neighborhood Youth Corps—by renaming it "Work and Training for Youth and Adults." In addition, the rewritten title provided authority, and money, for the Concentrated Employment Program, for a program to encourage involvement of private industry in training the disadvantaged, and for the new coordinating mechanism called the Comprehensive Work and Training Program. Operation Mainstream and the New Careers were transferred to the new Title I, removing them from the restrictions of Title II state allocation formulas and permitting closer coordination with the other manpower programs. The Special Impact program was more precisely defined, to tie it closer to area economic development.

The new amendments contained two other features designed to facilitate coordination. First, the Neighborhood Youth Corps lost its separate identification in the law and was split into two parts: a program to provide needy high school students with paid work experience both during the school year and in the summer; and a program to provide unemployed, underemployed, and low income "persons" (not limited to youth) with work experience and training to help them prepare for regular employment. This was a deliberate attempt by the Congress, fully supported by the Administration, to open up the type of work experience opportunities that prevailed in the Neighborhood Youth Corps to adults as well as youth. It was a recognition that paid "work experience" is a necessary component of a comprehensive manpower program and should be included in the range of services a local sponsor has to offer his clients if he is to be able to tailor his manpower program to individual needs.

However, removing the legislative barriers to flexible programming proved less difficult than changing local practice. To open up the ongoing Neighborhood Youth Corps projects to adults without additional funds would have meant cutting back on the numbers of youth being served in local projects—something that neither federal officials, particularly field representatives, nor local project sponsors would accept willingly. As a result, full use of this new authority has not been made—another illustration of the dangers inherent in categorical funding.

The second change in the Act which could affect coordination of local programs is the so-called Green Amendment.[16] This amendment requires that at least one-third of the boards of the Community Action Agencies be elected officials, and that a community action agency be a state, a political subdivision of a state, or a public or private nonprofit agency or organization which has been designated by a state or political subdivision of a state. In fact, the amendment was an invitation to mayors to take over local Community Action Agencies. As such, it holds considerable potential for a more efficient integration of manpower programs, particularly since the Model Cities program also vests control with the mayor or his representative.

It is still too early to say whether the Green Amendment will fulfill its potential as a force for coordination. In the first go-around, the mayors turned out to be somewhat less than enthusiastic about the prospect of taking over the Community Action Agencies, and more than 90 percent respectfully declined the invitation. Many mayors evidently felt that the Community Action Agencies provided a useful, even a necessary, buffer between themselves and the ghetto, and that to take over the CAA would be too great a political risk. Furthermore, since the CAAs were providing services to the poor that had not been provided before, there was a general reluctance to disturb existing machinery that was working, though sometimes inefficiently. However, the presence of elected officials and their representatives on the CAA boards may well lead to a gradual increase of control by mayors over manpower programs. This would not, of course, guarantee effective coordination, but it should improve the odds.

### The CEP

Although there was no legislative reference to the Concentrated Employment Program until the 1967 EOA amendments, by the time they were enacted in late 1967 the CEP was already well underway. As was noted earlier, however, the concept of resource concentration was included in the President's Manpower Message to the Congress in early 1967. That message responded

35

to the Special Unemployment Surveys of 1966 and to the report of the President's Committee on Manpower's three-man teams. It stated, first, that the bulk of the structural unemployment problem was concentrated in identifiable geographic areas or pockets of poverty; and, second, that no single manpower program or service was sufficient by itself to get at the multiple employment problems of the hard-core unemployed. CEP was the administration's answer to the concept of concentration. Basically, the CEP was designed to bring together in a single limited target area, in one contract with a single sponsor, the complete range of manpower programs and services a disadvantaged individual needs to move from unemployment and unemployability to a permanent job.

As early as 1966, the Department of Labor began to argue for the concentration of manpower resources in the areas of greatest need. In March 1966, when Secretary Wirtz testified before the House Committee on Education and Labor on the Poverty Program, he stated that a guiding principle for the poverty manpower program should be concentration: "These 'job creation and job training' programs must be *concentrated* in the areas where poverty is concentrated and must be devised to meet the clearly identified needs of the people in the areas."[17] The Special Unemployment Surveys gave the Labor Department the ammunition it needed to support the proposition, and included in the Department's FY 1968 budget submission to the Bureau of the Budget in late 1966 was a proposal for a concentrated employment program. President Johnson was persuaded of the correctness of this position and early in 1967 directed the Department of Labor to undertake the program, thereby providing the leverage needed to pull together the staff and the dollars to do the job.

The three-man teams were called to a meeting in February 1967 to discuss the next steps in the implementation of their reports. I went to the meeting and told the twenty-five to thirty men assembled in a basement conference room in the Department of Labor that the teams were to be dissolved, that we were starting a new program in nineteen cities and two rural areas, and that they were being assigned by their agencies to my office to work with local sponsors in those cities to develop a Concentrated Employment Program before the end of the fiscal year. For the first time, the Manpower Administration would have in each city a single federal presence—a manpower "czar"—responsible for putting together the disparate manpower programs into a cohesive whole.

We had the men for the job. Getting the money together was not so easy. As was usually the case with new programs launched at White House direction, program administrators were expected to get them underway with no new funds. This was due in part to the notion that a program successfully launched would attract favorable attention and its own funds from Congress the next year. It was also due to the belief, firmly held by the White House, and engendered by ever-present bureaucratic competition, that there is always some waste in ongoing programs, so that some water always can be squeezed out for a new seedling.

In any case, in order to start the CEP we had to scrape together approximately $100 million from the current year's manpower programs: from HEW, from the OEO, and from Labor. Neither HEW nor the OEO were very happy at the prospect of putting their money into the CEP, but with the White House behind it, HEW agreed to the use of some institutional MDTA funds, and OEO agreed to the use of delegated Economic Opportunity Act program funds. However, the Office of Economic Opportunity never came through with the Community Action Program funds that were supposed to be made available.

"Scraping together" in the federal bureaucracy takes a combination of toughness, dexterity, and hope that is a constant test of mettle and endurance. Toughness because you have to say no to good sponsors and projects; dexterity because you have to know how to shift funds around from one program to another; and hope because under the one year appropriation system, you never know for certain until the end of the year how much can be taken from ongoing projects for redistribution.[18] Of the $100 million, $48 million came from MDTA funds—about half "recaptured" from FY 1966 appropriations and half from unobligated FY 1967 funds. From the out-of-school Neighborhood Youth Corps program $13½ million was taken by cutting back on local projects that were not up to their authorized strength and did not seem likely to become so. The New Careers program, which was just getting underway and had a reserve of unobligated funds, contributed $19½ million; but all we could draw from Operation Mainstream—already fully committed—was $100,000. This left us with a $20 million gap if the program objectives were to be met.

The only untapped source was the Special Impact program (Title I-D of the Economic Opportunity Act), and although I was well aware that the CEP did not completely fit the concept of this program as it had been discussed on the Hill the year before, the decision to use Special Impact funds for the CEP was made with the full approval of the OEO, with the understanding that this would be a once-only abrogation of the legislative intent. It was also understood that the Bedford-Stuyvesant project—a complex of programs aimed at economic and manpower development in this large slum area of Brooklyn, New York—would be funded first. The remainder of Title I-D funds were to be made available for CEP.

The decision was not based solely on expediency. Senators Robert Kennedy and Jacob Javits had said repeatedly that they wanted the Special Impact program to be used to fill gaps that were not provided for in other programs—to do those things that were necessary to achieve a measurable impact on a community but that could not be done any other way. In the development of the first round of CEP projects, the Special Impact money was certainly used in this way—as glue money to hold together a comprehensive manpower program complete with all the components necessary to provide individuals with an unbroken sequence of manpower services.

As it turned out, only $17.5 million of the $25 million Title I-D funds was used for the CEP. However, in spite of the legislative mandate and OEO approval, there was a good deal of dissatisfaction on the Hill with our disposition of the Special Impact funds. The result was a rewrite of the Title I-D legislation in the 1967 amendments, and a partial withdrawal by OEO of the Department of Labor's authority over the operation of the program. Under an agreement, forced by the OEO, Labor was given only half of the funds for the Special Impact program. The fact that OEO had earlier concurred in the decision to use Title I-D in the CEP did not deter them from later joining in the general castigation of the Manpower Administration on this issue.

Another and perhaps more seriously damaging effect of the diversion of FY 1967 funds to CEP, and later of the FY 1968 funds to JOBS, was the series of amendments to the Manpower Development and Training Act in 1968 which considerably reduced the flexibility of the Manpower Administrator in the management of funds, and gave a greater degree of control to the states.

*Private Industry Involvement*

The President's call for increased involvement of private industry in manpower programs—the second major point in his 1967 manpower message—coincided completely with the interests and convictions of many congressmen and senators on both sides of the aisle. Senator Javits, particularly, had been pressing this point for some time. The amendment proposed by the Administration to encourage such involvement was therefore largely non-controversial. There was the usual concern on the part of the unions that funds authorized under this amendment would be used to subsidize low-wage, highly mobile, labor-intensive industries, but that concern was alleviated by a specific prohibition in the House report to prevent such an occurrence.[19] This has been a source of friction with some industrial leaders, especially in the early days of the National Alliance of Businessmen, when leaders of the apparel industry found their companies excluded from participation in government-sponsored manpower projects. However, the legislative history makes the intent of Congress very clear in this regard. The whole issue of private industry involvement in manpower programs and the development of the JOBS program and the National Alliance of Businessmen will be discussed in detail in a separate paper.

*The Comprehensive Work and Training Program (CWTP)*

Finally, President Johnson's 1967 message stressed the need to coordinate manpower programs at the local level. The 1967 Economic Opportunity Act amendments reflected this need by requiring local communities to plan manpower programs through a coordinating mechanism called the Comprehensive Work and Training Program. The CWTP requires that all of the manpower programs under Title I-B of the Act, except JOBS, be funded in a designated "community program area" by a "prime sponsor" who will be responsible for putting the programs together in a Comprehensive Work and Training Program.[20] Although CWTP was not originally an Administration proposal, the idea followed naturally from the CEP concept and CEP experience with a single sponsor for a comprehensive range of manpower programs and services in a clearly delineated target area. The CWTP amendment was offered by Senator Joseph Clark who had for a long time championed the cause of coordination.[21] Clark was also a strong supporter of the Community Action Agencies and saw the Comprehensive Work and Training Program as a useful bulwark against those who were determined to reduce CAA funds and flexibility. Clark wanted the law to specify that the prime sponsor should be a Community Action Agency, but the House did not accept this provision and it was not included in the final version of the bill. However, as discussed earlier, the delegation agreement between the Department of Labor and the Office of Economic Opportunity did specify that the Community Action Agency would be "the presumed sponsor" of Economic Opportunity Act manpower programs. As a result, most Economic Opportunity Act manpower programs are now sponsored by CAAs. In fact, in many areas, manpower is the biggest single item in the local CAA budget—providing much of the administrative support for the whole CAA operation.

These annual battles over the Economic Opportunity Act—taking from six to nine months yearly, of both legislators' and administrators' time, resulting in a series of cliff-hangers over the passage of "continuing resolutions" on which the life of the OEO and the poverty programs depended, necessitating an avalanche of paper work as thousands of individual contracts were modified and extended month by month and sometimes week by week, and exhausting everyone in the process—were finally too much to take. Mercifully, in 1967 the Economic Opportunity Act was extended for two years instead of the usual one, giving both the executive branch and the Congress a chance to catch up and concentrate on the improvement of administration, as well as on significant evaluation.

## WORK INCENTIVE PROGRAM (WIN)

The most recent important legislative development in the manpower area was the amendment to the Social Security Act of 1967 providing training and work opportunities for welfare recipients. As early as 1962, the administration was concerned about the rising welfare rolls. In city after city it became shockingly apparent that "welfare" was no longer a temporary means of support to help those made helpless through no fault of their own but a permanent trap with no escape. The discovery that third-generation welfare families were not unusual led to a determination to find a way to help people off welfare by preparing them for jobs.

The concept of enforced work as a condition for receipt of welfare benefits is unacceptable to most people. When the city manager of Newburg, New York, tried it, he brought down a storm of disapprobation on himself and the city. But providing the opportunity for work on a voluntary basis, through training and work experience, meets more readily with public approval.

Accordingly, in 1962 the Social Security Act was amended to authorize a program of community work and training for welfare recipients, particularly where there was an unemployed but employable parent living at home. It was hoped that this program would give additional encouragement to the states to take advantage of the option in the law added in 1961 to extend their AFDC programs (Aid to Families with Dependent Children) to cover families where there were needy children as a result of the unemployment of the parents. Because of the cost and the fifty-fifty matching requirements, however, by 1964 only eighteen states had taken advantage of the new amendment. The Work Experience and Training Program under Title V of the Economic Opportunity Act (the "Happy Pappy program"), with much more favorable matching provisions for the states (originally 100 percent federal funds, it was reduced to 80 to 20 percent by a later amendment), was designed to supplement the lagging Community Work and Training Program (CWT) of the Social Security Act.

In view of the general discussion today on the proper relationship of work and training programs to welfare, and a growing recognition that the present welfare system may be contributing to the disruption of the family structure, it is interesting to note that the early name of the Title V Work Experience program was "Family Unity Through Jobs."[22]

As the program was explained to the Congress, the idea was to provide employment assistance to unemployed fathers not covered by the existing welfare programs and thereby prevent the disintegration of family units. "The Family Unity Through Jobs program has been designed to encourage the expansion of existing programs, the establishment of new AFDC—Unemployed Parent programs, and the inclusion of work and training programs on a pilot basis where they do not now exist."[23] The proposed budget for this program was $150 million, of which $130 million was to be used for jobs and training for unemployed fathers not eligible for public assistance, $12 million for jobs and training for unemployed fathers who were eligible for public assistance, and only $8 million for training for welfare mothers.[24] In practice, it was not possible to limit the program to unemployed fathers, and almost half of Title V enrollees were females.

By 1967, it was clear that the legislation on the books was not adequate to meet the employment problems of welfare recipients. We were not getting the welfare clients into MDTA; the Community Work and Training Program of the Social Security Act was too expensive for the states; and the Title V program, which had been broadened to include "other needy persons," was not getting at the welfare problem.

Early in 1967 there were discussions at the White House on a bill to provide work incentives for welfare clients. Secretary Wirtz and I made strong representations that such a program was a manpower program and should be administered by the Department of Labor along with other manpower programs. Secretary Wilbur Cohen of HEW took the position that it should be in his department. He argued that the welfare worker needed to be able to offer something besides a check; that the interagency complications of referring people from the welfare office to the Employment Service were too complicated; that welfare clients needed the case work approach dealing with the whole family and not with just one segment of the family's problems; and that, in any case, if the Department of Labor wanted the program, they would have to keep it separate, with separate funding under special legislation. Given the temper of the times, Secretary Cohen's condition would have made it difficult, if not impossible, to obtain necessary funds. Congress, which would not have looked favorably on a brand new budget item, might have scuttled the whole idea.

We argued the necessity of pulling all manpower programs together and suggested that far from ruling out the case-worker approach, we intended to adopt that system. Employment Service counselors and job specialists would work as a team tailoring an employability and training program to each individual's special needs and abilities.

Our view prevailed, and the White House decided to put the whole program in the Department of Labor. At this point the program was called WIP, standing for Work Incentive Program. Later, when the opposition used the name to describe what they believed the program would do to welfare recipients, Secretary

43

Wirtz changed the name to WIN, obviously a much more hopeful and promising designation for any new program.

The Department of Labor almost lost the program during the long discussions and negotiations on the Hill. At one point several of the state Employment Security administrators appeared and testified at a key executive session of the House Ways and Means Committee. As Chairman Wilbur Mills later reported to a group from the Interstate Conference of State Employment Security Agencies, the apathetic tone of the Employment Service witnesses at that meeting, defending the past record of the Employment Service and showing no real initiative or concern with the future, convinced the Committee—which had previously been in favor of giving the program to Labor—that it should be administered by HEW instead. However, Congressman Mills did indicate his willingness to cooperate if we could get the Senate to accept the Department of Labor. The Senate Finance Committee, chaired by Senator Russell Long of Louisiana, was persuaded that all of the manpower programs should be in one place, and in the final conference version the House accepted the Senate position.

## WAGNER-PEYSER ACT

No discussion of the legislative base for the manpower programs would be complete without mention of the Wagner-Peyser Act of 1933, establishing the federal-state Employment Service system. The Wagner-Peyser Act, which for more than thirty years has without substantial revision provided the authority for the operations of the Employment Service system, is based on two principles which tend to make the integration of manpower policy difficult, and sometimes impossible. First, the Act assumes that the Employment Service must provide services to all, to whoever asks for them. Strictly interpreted, this could mean that there should not be a concentration of effort on the disadvantaged. In the sixties, particularly, we rejected that interpretation; nevertheless, it was, and remains, one of the reasons why it has been so difficult to redirect the effort of the Employment Service.

The second principle is reliance upon the states as the operating arm of the system. The argument has revolved around the degree of independence that the 100 percent federally funded state agencies should have in the conduct of national policy. I believe that the problem here is not a constitutional one but an administrative one involving the method of financing.

SUMMARY

In this chapter I have tried to trace the development of the different laws that make up the present manpower program. Some are there because of the strong views and special interests of particular representatives and senators (Operation Mainstream, New Careers, and the Special Impact programs, for example). Some evolved from a long history of pressure from a variety of sources, coming to a head at a particular time (the Neighborhood Youth Corps and the JOBS programs). Some resulted when administrative experience made changes in direction and content almost inevitable (the WIN, the CEP, and the evolutionary amendments to the MDTA). Together, these programs make up a remarkable manpower system—but a system that has built-in contradictions, overlap, and duplication.

# 3

## Manpower Planning and Resource Allocation

Effective program coordination begins, of course, with systematic planning; but, as we have seen, planning for manpower suffers more from too many partial systems than from a total lack of system.

As early as 1966, the Manpower Administration began to press for a workable and comprehensive planning system. In order to provide the states with a blueprint for the redirection of the MDTA to the disadvantaged, we initiated what was then called the National State Manpower Development Plan. The Manpower Administration, working with HEW, drew up guidelines for the states to develop specific plans for all MDTA institutional and on-the-job training programs. States were asked to set up coordinating committees to assist them in the development of the state and local plans. When the plans were completed they were to be reviewed by a national committee of representatives of Labor, HEW, and Commerce. Limited experience with this rudimentary planning system led to the decision, the next year, to broaden its scope and include all federally aided manpower programs, not just the MDTA. Similarly, the planning group was expanded to include all of the

46

federal agencies administering manpower or related programs, as well as their counterparts at the state and local levels. The result was the Cooperative Area Manpower Planning System (CAMPS), launched in March 1967, with seven federal agencies signing the original agreement, including the Department of Labor; the Welfare Administration, Vocational Rehabilitation, and Vocational Education (all under the Department of Health, Education, and Welfare); the Office of Economic Opportunity; the Economic Development Administration of the Department of Commerce; and the Department of Housing and Urban Development.[1] By March 1968, four additional agencies had joined the system; the Bureau of Indian Affairs and the Water Pollution Control Administration of the Department of the Interior; the Department of Agriculture; and the Civil Service Commission.

Of the eleven signatory agencies to the basic CAMPS agreement, three represent constituent bureaus of HEW, and two, constituent bureaus of the Department of Interior. This is because there was no single source in either department willing to assume responsibility for committing their respective departments to CAMPS. As a result, both the Department of Labor and the Office of Economic Opportunity can speak with one voice on the national committee, while HEW—which sends three representatives to the committee, each protecting separate interests—cannot.

CAMPS is basically a system of counterpart committees, federal, state, and local, with the state committee in the swing position. The structure starts with approximately 400 local area planning committees. (Although the national CAMPS coordinating committee designated only about 100 area committees, one for each of the major job market areas, or SMSA's, many state committees have extended the program to additional local areas.) In theory, these committees are to assess the needs of the area for manpower and related supportive services, to balance those needs against all available resources, to determine priorities for the allocation of resources, and to see that local efforts are coordinated to deal with the priority requirements. The local plan is passed on to a state committee, which must put local area plans together

47

with an overall state plan after adjusting needs to available resources. This state plan is forwarded to a regional CAMPS committee, made up of regional representatives of the signatory federal agencies and chaired by the Regional Manpower Administrator. Approval authority for the state plans lies with the regional committee. The national CAMPS committee is the collector of the total sum of the state plans and the overseer of the operations of the system.

Although CAMPS has the potential for becoming a sophisticated planning system, as it is presently constituted there are at least four basic defects inhibiting its development.

First, it is a cooperative, voluntary arrangement at best, dependent on a collective will that is sometimes hard to find.

There was some question in the beginning as to what the "C" should stand for. It ought to have been for "comprehensive," but without authority to make it so, it had to be for "cooperative." As the system branches outward from federal to state to local levels, it tends to become progressively *less* comprehensive, and more dependent on voluntarism.

While federal officials are required to take part in the CAMPS process, and, in fact, federal program representation rather than community participation has been the guiding principal for membership, each committee also includes voluntary representation from state and local agencies. Many of those originally invited to become members of the CAMPS committee, unsure of their responsibility to the committee and of the committee's value to their operations, attended the first few meetings and then delegated the assignment to subordinates. As a result, turnover on the committees has been high and continuity hard to achieve. Others who were invited have never accepted membership, convinced from the start that CAMPS held nothing for them.

Second, CAMPS is not comprehensive. It has no real authority for the allocation of resources to manpower programs except for the MDTA institutional program and a part of the OJT program. Resources for manpower programs under the Economic Opportunity Act and the Work Incentive Program have not been subjected to allocation through CAMPS but have been distributed to local sponsors on the basis of prior decisions made in Washington. Even authority over MDTA is questioned on occasion. At least one State Employment Service agency has taken the position that the state constitution prohibits delegation of the planning authority for MDTA to a committee.

When each of the categorical manpower program "pies" is divided in Washington into state and local pieces, the tidbits that end up on the local planning group tables are so small that neither a well-balanced diet nor a nourishing meal is possible. Practically all that is left for the local planners to do is to copy down the figures as they get them from the regional offices. Instead of being able to build a comprehensive manpower program tailored to community needs, the only kind of choice left to the planners is whether to have a class for clerk-typists or a class for nurse's aides, or whether the Neighborhood Youth Corps program should be in one school or two. The mix of programs has already been set on the basis of the division and subdivision of the limited number of dollars in the separate categorical pots.

The ability of the CAMPS committees to build comprehensive plans is further frustrated by the unwillingness or inability of other federal agencies in the system to submit their programs to the CAMPS process—particularly those programs for services in support of manpower such as health, basic or remedial education, economic development, and so on. These agencies have generally seen in CAMPS an opportunity to learn about other federal programs, a possible chance to obtain additional funds in support of their own programs, and a useful clearing-house for the exchange of information about local activities with colleagues whom they have often not even met before. They have not seen CAMPS as a proper body to which authority over their own resources should be relinquished. On the other hand, they have been pleased to take part in the determination as to how MDTA dollars should be spent.

In addition, technical problems such as the lack of timely information on the availability of resources, and separate planning cycles and deadlines for the different programs, have made comprehensive planning virtually impossible even with the best will in the world. In June 1969, with the start of the new fiscal year less than a month away, the FY 1970 guidelines still had not been distributed to state and local committees. Yet plans were supposed to be completed and in to the regional offices by July 15. Here is another example: the state Employment Service agencies are required to prepare an annual Plan of Service—a complete outline of what services the agency will provide in the next year, where they will be provided, and by whom. In theory, the Plan of Service should reflect as nearly as possible the local CAMPS manpower plan. But the planning cycle for the Plans of Service does not coincide with the CAMPS planning cycle—the deadline for submission of the Plan of Service having already passed before the work on the CAMPS even gets underway.

Third, there is an unreal quality in the CAMPS process that tends to make procedure more important than program. The immediate need for a comprehensive planning system is not clear to those who are expected to take part in the process. So long as the resources for manpower programs are inadequate to the total need, there appears to be little urgency or significance in such an elaborate system to match resources and needs. It is not, as Mr. Moynihan says, that the community planners have been plunged into a paralyzing trauma with the realization that everything relates to everything, but rather that they know that in the real world hardly anything relates to anything.[2] Programs are so small in proportion to need that the impact is minimal, and the danger of tripping over someone's else's program is not the major problem. In any case, what has occurred in many cities is an *ad hoc* arrangement in which each of the would-be competitors for the manpower action has staked out his own turf where each operates without any relation to the others. Agencies such as the Employment Service, the Community Action Agency, the Opportunities Industrialization Center, and others, have developed a *modus vivendi* and for the most part do not get in each other's way. The problems come whenever there is an addition to the resources being made available in a community. Then, of course, each group competes with the others. By and large, these agencies are glad to use the CAMPS to find out what the others are doing, but they do not regard CAMPS as the arena within which to fight for the prize.

Another aspect of the unreal nature of CAMPS is the imprecise organizational arrangements evidenced by the tremendous variation, in size, composition, and function in both state and local committees. Some committees are very large (over 100), some very small (only 3 or 4). Some have advisory bodies, some do not. Most do no real planning; they only rubberstamp the final document prepared, generally, by the staff of the local Employment Service agency. However, there are instances where a CAMPS committee has forced a change in a member agency's plans. In one case, for example, the CAMPS committee required the vocational education agency to offer training courses taught in Spanish in a Puerto Rican neighborhood previously unserved by the agency.

Finally, the interest of state and local officials in the committee chairmanships represents another example of the small significance attributed to CAMPS. In the first year, chairmanship of both state and local committees was with Employment Service staff. The next year, however, it was decided that elected officials—the governors and the mayors—should be more involved. Letters were sent to the governors asking them to take charge if they so desired. Most state committees, however, remain chaired by the head of the state Employment Security agency. In fact, he is often the man designated by the governor. In some cases (e.g., Maryland, New Jersey, Utah, Iowa, and Michigan), the governor has designated a person operating directly out of his own office. In California, the chairman is the head of the new State Human Resources Agency. In at least one state, the chairman is the head of the Economic Development agency.

The pattern in the area committees is even more diffuse. Like the governors, who do not appear to see the value in a system that does not exercise much authority, the mayors have not responded to the invitation to take over the local CAMPS committees. Where there are Human Resource agencies, the head of that agency has become the chairman of the CAMPS committee; but in most cases, perhaps 65 to 70 percent of the committees, the local chairman is the local Employment Service area manager. In at least one city where the city Human Resources administration is in charge, the animosity between the local committee and the state committee was so great that the local committee refused to send its plan to the state, and as a result never submitted a plan at all. Needless to say, the city was a large and important one and its projects were funded in spite of the fact that there was no plan.

The fourth defect in the CAMPS system is related to operations rather than design. From the beginning it was clear that a good job of planning would require expert staff support that was not then available to the participants. Carryover MDTA money was made available and staff positions allocated to the states for CAMPS planning in FY 1968, with the understanding that new funds and positions would be requested in FY 1969. This was done, but the request was turned down by the House Appropriations Committee. After some negotiation, however, agreement was reached in the conference committee that regular MDTA dollars could be diverted for this purpose. Staff positions were then allocated to the state Employment Security agencies. Planning staffs, of course, were expected to report to the committee chairman, but were to be under the administrative supervision of the state agencies, and with few exceptions were to be selected under state merit systems. As a result, almost all of the CAMPS staff work has been done in the state agencies. This year, however, money for staffing CAMPS operations has been offered directly to the governors as a further incentive to them to take a more active role.

It occurs to me that this could turn out to be nothing more than a political slush fund for the governors—not because of insidious intent on the part of the administrators of the manpower program but because CAMPS itself, as it is presently operating, is so far from being a meaningful planning process, is so disconnected from reality, that the work of putting a so-called plan together is a futile

52

exercise. If CAMPS is as it seems—represented by a shelf full of xeroxed paper constituting a nonplan, read by no one, and useful only as a reminder that the medium should *not* be the message— then the problems of providing staff are decidedly secondary to the need for a complete rethinking of the whole planning process.

## Comprehensive Work and Training Program (CWTP)

There were times during my tenure as Manpower Administrator when it seemed that the people concerned with manpower programs and policy were divided into two distinct groups, pre-poverty and post-poverty, inhabiting separate worlds and not only completely scornful of the significance of the other but loath to admit each other's existence. Even within the Manpower Administration, the different bureaus often had this kind of attitude toward each other. So it was with the development of a manpower planning system. CAMPS is the creature of the MDTA crowd (essentially the pre-poverty group, who cut their teeth on the Overall Economic Development Program concept of the Area Redevelopment Act), while the Comprehensive Work and Training Program is the creature of the Economic Opportunity Act crowd (the post-poverty group).

Like CAMPS, CWTP is designed to make manpower programs more responsive to local needs and to provide a mechanism for coordination and integration of local manpower efforts. As stated earlier, CWTP is a planning and delivery system, built into the 1967 Economic Opportunity Act amendments, requiring that certain manpower programs in a designated community program area be planned by and funded through a designated prime sponsor.[3] Before the Comprehensive Work and Training Program could be put into effect, four issues had to be resolved.

1. How much of the total manpower program could reasonably be expected to be covered through the CWTP?
2. How should a program area be defined? Should it be limited to the target area concept of the CEP, citywide, labor market area, or larger?

3. Who should be the prime sponsor, and how should he be selected?
4. What would be the relationship of the CWTP to other manpower programs and systems, particularly CAMPS and the CEP?

The first issue was relatively simple to decide, and, in fact, the Congress itself recognized that the CWTP amendment would initially have to be limited to Title I-B programs except for JOBS.[4] It was quickly agreed that it would not be useful or politic to require the newly formed National Alliance of Businessmen to submit "their" JOBS program to a community planning and delivery system. Furthermore, the time was not propitious for the new legislation which would be necessary to bring MDTA into the new planning system.

The last three were tough issues—with several difficult hurdles impeding their resolution. First, there were the disagreements between the Office of Economic Opportunity and the Department of Labor, and the long negotiations on the delegation of authority for the Economic Opportunity Act programs. Second, there were organizational problems within the Manpower Administration itself. And finally, the State Employment Security agencies, supported by the Bureau of Employment Security, were anxious to delay implementation as long as possible in the hope that delay would result in upsetting the concept behind the Comprehensive Work and Training Program and allow the state agencies to win out over the community action agencies as prime sponsors.

All during the period of the development of manpower programs for the disadvantaged, there was a continuing struggle between the Office of Economic Opportunity and the Department of Labor over the role of the state Employment Service agencies and the Community Action Agencies vis-à-vis manpower programs. The Employment Service cause was championed with great fervor by the Bureau of Employment Security. Ardent CAA support came from the Community Action Program division of OEO. Both sides recognized the importance of manpower in the nascent drive for community development. Both correctly saw manpower as the key to control and power in the urban ghetto areas. Each time the struggle came to a head—as it did repeatedly—it was resolved by a series of compromises that tried to give a part of the action to both groups. There were always, of course, individual staff members in both agencies who felt that their side was being sold out. But it was always my feeling that there was, and is, a legitimate role for both the Employment Service and the CAAs. If the Employment Service is to become the chief operating arm of national manpower policy, as I think it must, then it must change its attitudes and practices. But it could not, and will not, change to meet the needs of the disadvantaged without constant pressure to force such a change. Part of the pressure can come from the Community Action Agencies which—despite their limitations—effectively voice the aspirations of the poor. In 1967 the CAA's were developing a capability of reaching the disadvantaged that the Employment Service did not have. Therefore, I saw the two agencies as complementing each other, in a constructive competition that could result in better service to those who needed it.

The bureaucratic struggles on this issue were not just on the interagency level between the Office of Economic Opportunity and the Department of Labor. Even within Labor, there was a difference of opinion as to what the role of the Employment Service should be. Generally, the new people who came into the Manpower Administration with the advent of the antipoverty manpower programs tended to feel that the Employment Service was hopelessly out of date, and that its role in the new programs should be severely limited. They did not want to eliminate the Employment Service, but they were not at all sympathetic to any move that would give the Employment Service additional authority or resources. On the other hand, the leaders of the Employment Service —especially Frank Cassell and Charles Odell—felt that it would take clear authority and additional resources to update and reorient it to current problems and to utilize the expertise developed over the years.

It is not surprising, then, that when the delegation agreement between the Office of Economic Opportunity and the Department

55

of Labor was finally completed in March 1968, making the Community Action Agencies the prime sponsors of the Economic Opportunity Act Title I-B programs, the state Employment Security agencies represented by the Interstate Conference of Employment Security Agencies (ICESA) and the Bureau of Employment Security were very unhappy. I felt that if we were to move ahead and fully implement the Comprehensive Work and Training amendment, the Employment Service would have to be persuaded to give up its obstructionist tactics and work more constructively toward assuming the responsibilities which the new laws gave to it.

In early 1968, at a meeting of the Urban Affairs Committee of the Interstate Conference this is, in effect, what I told them.[5] Malcolm Lovell[6] and R. L. Coffman, the state administrators for Michigan and Texas, respectively, called me out of the meeting to propose that the Executive Committee of the ICESA take up the matter. I did not think the Executive Committee would be receptive to anything I had to offer. As an alternative I suggested to Lovell and Coffman that the Urban Affairs Committee of the Interstate Conference take on the job and work directly with the Manpower Administration to develop procedures for the implementation of the Comprehensive Work and Training Program. They agreed, and from then on the Urban Affairs Committee, chaired by Alfred Green, Employment Security Administrator for New York, met weekly with the top staff of the Manpower Administration to work out detailed procedures. Meanwhile the dilatory tactics of the groups within the Manpower Administration unsympathetic to the CWTP were overcome primarily by the threat of congressional displeasure over noncompliance with the law. Although we could not meet the deadline stipulated in the law, requiring that all I-B programs be included in a CWTP and funded through designated prime sponsors by July 1, 1968, we were able to get an extension from Congress on the promise to move ahead with the plan. In October 1968, a manpower order was issued, setting the guidelines for the implementation of CWTP.[7] This order went one step further than the delegation agreement and stipulated that for I-B programs, the Community Action Agency *is* the sponsor instead of being the presumed sponsor. The Employment Service was given equal billing and *is* the deliverer of manpower services. In my opinion, the order represents a real step toward the goal of making the Employment Service a constructive force for social change by establishing, for the first time, the right of a local group to monitor and evaluate the performance of the local agency. The fact that this was accomplished in cooperation and full agreement with the Urban Affairs Committee of the Interstate Conference of Employment Security Agencies is especially significant.

Although the Comprehensive Work and Training Program may leave something to be desired as a planning mechanism for local manpower programs, the requiring of single sponsorship could be a big step forward in bringing about better coordination of local programs. The defects of the CWTP are more in the incompleteness of coverage, in the lack of a clear definition of a community planning area, and in a lack of understanding of its function at the local level then in the design for delivery of manpower services.

It should be noted, however, that the CWTP is still not operative. Some of the same barriers to implementation that existed when the amendment was enacted still exist and have been reinforced by the announced intention of the present administration to utilize state machinery—as opposed to community or city machinery—for planning and operation of manpower and other social programs.

## MODEL CITIES AS A PLANNING SYSTEM

The third federally sponsored manpower planning mechanism is the Model Cities organization, but its relationship to the CWTP and CAMPS has not yet been rationalized. If the Model Cities program evolves into the primary vehicle for urban community development, as is expected by its chief supporters, it could provide the basis for a fully integrated manpower planning system as a piece of total development plan.

The hard problems that arise in connection with the Model

Cities program vis-à-vis manpower planning are due to the fact that planning is done by the major groups involved independently of each other, and to the time lag that frequently exists between the initiation of manpower programs in a target area and the initiation of the total Model Cities program. Let me cite a few examples.

In a major eastern city the manpower component of the Model Cities program has been developed independently of everything else that is already going on in the target area, and there is quite a lot going on. The local Community Action Agency has, in addition to a large Concentrated Employment Program, several other manpower programs in the same area, some by courtesy of the Department of Labor, some by courtesy of the OEO. But there is much more. A recent survey turned up over one hundred private and public manpower and manpower related programs in the same area. However, though the Model Cities program is planned for target areas that coincide with the CEP target areas, the Model Cities manpower component is completely unrelated to the other manpower programs there. It is even based on a different ideological concept than ongoing programs, namely, that there must be upgrading of the near-poor (primarily the low-income whites) before further employment advances can be made for the poor (primarily blacks and Puerto Ricans). Unfortunately, the plan for this city is so ill defined that none of the present actors on the manpower scene feels compelled to take it seriously. But it is apparent that sooner or later there must be a reconciliation of the separate plans.

In another city the manpower component of the Model Cities plan has been carefully designed to utilize all existing resources. In this case, it makes up one-seventh of a well-integrated program, with each piece interrelated and interdependent. This city is neither a CEP nor a JOBS city, however, which means that at present there are no manpower dollars specifically earmarked for it.[8] Without additional manpower appropriations, there is little likelihood that the manpower component of the Model Cities program can be funded. Without the manpower component, the balance of this integrated Model Cities plan suffers; certainly it changes character, and perhaps it becomes worthless.

In a third, medium-sized industrial city, the energetic mayor has done exceptionally well in getting federal funds for his programs. The city has everything: CEP, JOBS, an Urban Renewal program, and it is a Model City. The mayor feels that good planning is the key to his success in getting federal programs into the area. Yet there are several planning groups operating in the city and one of his problems is to get them working together; he is presently trying to combine some of the staffs. But the city civil service system, which controls state jobs, doesn't give him the flexibility he needs to staff up (and down) for the one-time crash planning demanded by most federal programs.

These examples point up one of the major issues that must be resolved if there is to be effective implementation of manpower policy. The failure to tie the manpower programs to Model Cities is not due to the usual Washington bureaucratic secrecy and squabbling, or to any lack of will to cooperate between government departments, but to the real complexities involved in bringing off a grand-scale integration of several kinds of community rehabilitation programs in a federal-state-local system. Every effort was made in the Department of Labor and the Manpower Administration to tie manpower programs to Model Cities. Interdepartmental review teams were established. Manpower Administration staff participated in meetings around the country with the mayors of potential Model Cities to assist them with proposals. A policy was adopted that would make the CEP a part of the Model Cities program to the extent that resources would permit.

If the Model Cities program is indeed to be given top national priority and become the chosen instrument for the rehabilitation of our cities, a status which neither the Johnson nor the Nixon Administration has accorded it, then that decision must be backed by a determination to make the local Model Cities agency the lead local planning group, and by sufficient authority to command the range of federal resources necessary to translate approved plans into efficient operations.

## RESOURCE ALLOCATION

An important part—indeed a vital part—of an effective planning system is timely information on the availability of resources. It is all well and good to add up the needs of a community and to plan a program to meet those needs. But if there is no indication of the extent of resources to meet the needs, the planning is useless. A good example of what can happen when planning is not realistically related to potential resources occurred in the first round of the Concentrated Employment Program.

After the initial nineteen CEP cities were selected, there was considerable discussion in Manpower Administration staff sessions as to whether these cities should be told what funds were available to them before they prepared project proposals. We finally decided to withhold such information, not only because we were still not completely sure of the exact amounts but also because we felt that such information would result in a stereotyped CEP design that would not represent the thinking or real needs of the communities involved.

Chicago was one of the first cities to come in with its CEP proposal, drawn in haste, but representing some considerable effort by perhaps as many as one hundred people. The proposal added up to more than $80 million. The total funds actually available for the entire CEP—nineteen cities and two rural areas—was $100 million, which was divided into five separate and fairly restrictive categories.

The disparity between the Chicago proposal and a program that could be approved was so great that the only thing to do was to start over, but with a serious handicap, since the end of the fiscal year was then only a few weeks away. Paring down the original was out of the question. Precious time had been lost, effort wasted, tempers frayed, and frustration was evident on all sides. The proposal that was approved in the final hours of the fiscal year did not, of course, do much more than meet the minimum specifications and match the money available. As a result, it was months before the Chicago CEP could become operative. Needless to say, the Chicago experience was not repeated with the other CEP cities.

Not only is it important to make sure that local planners know the approximate amount that will be available for planning purposes, but such information must be in their hands well ahead of the time when programs are to start operating if planning is to have any meaning at all. The lack of timely information is a problem that has plagued manpower program administrators at every level for some time. Continuation of such a situation will result in a waste of effort and time that no business could afford to tolerate. At least one of the villains of this particular story is the congressional requirement that authorizations and appropriations be for one year only. When appropriations are made long after the beginning of the year in which the money is to be spent, the barriers to effective administration are compounded and the situation becomes little short of ridiculous. There have been times when an annual appropriation for manpower programs has come almost six months after the beginning of the operating year. To expect any kind of realistic advance planning—related to more or less firm allocations of resources—to be done under these circumstances is not only unrealistic but unfair to the people who have that responsibility.

One possible solution is for program administrators to make a reasonable estimate of resource availability, and this is usually done. But when manpower programs grow at such a rapid rate, when new programs are added each year, "reasonable" estimates are hard to come by. In addition, when it is necessary to shift national priorities, as was the case in 1967 in the decision to go to a CEP approach, and again in 1968 in the decision to increase private industry involvement through the JOBS program and the National Alliance of Businessmen, the confidence of planners in estimated resources is seriously undermined. After a few experiences of this sort, the tendency of the planners is to go ahead anyway, knowing that their work may be completely irrelevant, but justifying their existence by putting out paper and meeting deadlines on the theory that something is better than nothing. The paper world becomes the reality—completely separate from the system of actual appropriations, distribution of real money, and operating projects.

Resource allocation problems are not limited to the area of management or appropriation schedules. They go much deeper than that. The basic problem is the double standard that the Congress has forced upon the executive branch, which makes sensible administration almost impossible. In short, the same committees of Congress have mandated two separate systems of resource allocation—one to the states through the MDTA, and one to local sponsors through the EOA. The development of separate planning and delivery systems is a direct result of the legislative requirements for the different systems of resource allocation. The same people who are responsible for laying out two roads going in opposite directions now wonder why the Executive Branch, and particularly the Department of Labor, can't seem to get all the drivers to the agreed upon destination in a neat and tidy way.

This congressionally created difficulty has been intensified by the natural frictions that exist between state and local agencies when each sees the other with a source of federal wealth, the access to which is off limits for one or the other. State agencies are not happy when local agencies can have a line into a federal source of supply that is out of reach for them, as is the case with the funds for manpower programs under Title I-B of the Economic Opportunity Act. On the other hand, local agencies such as the city governments and the Community Action Agencies dislike having to go to state agencies in order to get the kind of manpower dollars they need to round out their programs, especially when the two levels may be further divided by a difference in political control—for example, when there is a Democratic mayor and a Republican governor.

When the federal dollars are distributed in what appears to be a capricious fashion, no one has the authority or the means to force an effective coordination of all the components of a comprehensive manpower system. Persuasion and voluntary cooperation become the only cards in the would be coordinator's hand—and neither is exactly what could be called the ace of trump.

Until the Congress is willing to face up to this issue, and to the necessity for simplifying the basic procedures for the allocation of resources, the frictions between state and local levels of government will not be improved, at least in the manpower area, and realistic coordination of local programs will remain a never ending task.

# 4

## Manpower Operations—
## Who's Got the Action?

The inconsistent pattern of manpower operations that has developed at the local level can be traced to the tremendous infusion of new manpower programs and money over a relatively short period of time, to the competing and often conflicting bureaucratic interests at every level of government, and to the haphazard layering of one planning and/or delivery system on top of another. But it is also due to the great variations in the political and social structure of local communities. The federal-state-local relationship presents an enormous range of community organizations. Each state, each community is different, and in consequence each develops an operating or delivery system that reflects its own needs and strengths. Personalities, special interests, and institutional structure all play a part in setting the pattern for the operation of local manpower programs, just as they do for other social and economic programs.

The problems of local coordination surface in different places in different ways, making it difficult to pull together manpower program components into an integrated system; to link separate manpower programs together in the best possible use of local institutional strengths and capabilities; or to tie manpower projects into broader economic and social community rehabilitation programs.

## PULLING MANPOWER PROGRAM COMPONENTS TOGETHER

The Concentrated Employment Program represents the high mark of the federal government's effort to coordinate the separate manpower programs at the local level in a sensible delivery system that would utilize local capabilities to the maximum extent. But the story of the erosion and apparent decline of the CEP is a good illustration of the natural anticoordination forces that exist in every community.

The struggle at the local level, insofar as manpower is concerned, is a struggle for a piece of the action—the larger the piece, the fiercer the struggle. For any one group in a community, coordination is almost by definition antithetical to satisfactory resolution of that struggle. The most obvious antagonists are, of course, the state Employment Service agency and the Community Action Agency. But there are many other groups involved: the city, employers, unions, and minority groups, to name a few.

The CEP has been under attack from its inception precisely because it requires separate community groups to submerge their special interests in the greater good. Although the roles of the Community Action Agency and the Employment Service were theoretically spelled out in guidelines from Washington, in practice each community has had to work out the arrangement that best fits its needs. In some CEP's the Employment Service has taken over all of the counseling and testing functions, and not much more. In others, Employment Service people are "outstationed" in the CEP, doing job development and placement, while counseling is done by CAA personnel or some other group. (In one state the state administrator has pulled the Employment Service staff out of the CEP and refused to work with it at all.)

The CEP got off to a good start because there was a single strong control at the top, and the necessary flexibility to adapt the program to local conditions. It is really a remarkable achievement that the CEP got underway in only four months—from the announcement in March 1967 to signed contracts in nineteen cities and two rural areas by June 30. This achievement surely deserves to be remembered in bureaucratic annals; it stands in contrast to the protracted and painful beginnings of the one-stop centers, or the Neighborhood Center Pilot Program (NCPP).

In August 1966, President Johnson made a speech in Syracuse, New York, saying that there ought to be one place in every ghetto in each of our major cities where poor people could go to get all of the kinds of help they needed: health services, employment and training assistance, legal services, education, consumer advice, family planning, and so on. The President asked Secretary Weaver of the Department of Housing and Urban Development to set as his goal the establishment of such a center in every major city in the nation. The Departments of HEW and Labor and the Office of Economic Opportunity were to work with HUD on this program. However, even with White House prestige and pressure behind the program, it took more than a year to get the federal agencies involved to agree to procedures for its initiation. By the fall of 1967, although fourteen cities had been selected for a pilot effort, planning had begun in only eleven of them. By the end of 1968, more than two years after Johnson's announcement, the plans for all but one of the cities had been approved. Although the program was operational in all thirteen approved cities in early 1969, it consisted primarily of a limited number of single service projects. Only two of the centers have new manpower components and new manpower funds.*

The problem with the Neighborhood Center Pilot Program was that it had no single point of authority or control. None of the four federal agencies involved was willing, or felt able, to relinquish its program dollars to another, and no single agency had the authority to force the others to put their money into the program.

* There is an ironic but apt postscript to the NCPP story. Like most federal programs, NCPP had its contract investigators and evaluators, in this case a prestigious New England social research firm. The result of its study is a 4,500 page report—4,500 pages about a program that, after three years, is only beginning to help poor people. In contrast, more than 155,600 persons have been enrolled in CEP in a two-year period. In the month of April 1969, over 70,000 were being given assistance in 79 CEP centers.

In the CEP, on the other hand, control over the money was in one agency with the result that "togetherness" could be, and was, enforced. If the local groups would not work together, they were not funded. With that kind of leverage the Community Action Agencies, the Employment Service, and other groups such as the Opportunities Industrialization Centers, the Urban League, or SER (a Mexican-American group) could be persuaded to work with each other and to accept the contributions the others could make. It was not easy to get all of them together, and in some cases federal intervention had to take a very positive form. In Newark, for instance, when CEP negotiations between the business community, the Community Action Agency, and the mayor seemed deadlocked, Bert Harding of the Office of Economic Opportunity and I flew there and made it clear that there would be no CEP unless everyone involved agreed to work together. That did the trick. A new organization incorporating all interests was formed; the Newark CEP was approved and is still operating.

Each local group likes best to do its own thing unhampered by any requirement to cooperate or work with others, and it is apparent that the pressure necessary to initiate a CEP must be maintained if it is to continue. In CEP the centrifugal forces have been stronger than the centripetal.

Indeed, the program has been subject to a constant erosion and spin-off from its beginning, with the constituencies of the separate categorical programs crying foul of the others, and taking steps to protect their own special operational preserves. One by one the program resources originally included in CEP have fallen away. The 1967 CEP program included, among other resources, Neighborhood Youth Corps and Operation Mainstream money. Plans for FY 1968 contemplated using additional money from these sources for new CEP's. But because projects in both programs had been shortfunded in the previous year, commitments had already been made that would have been hard to break, and as a result, no Neighborhood Youth Corps funds were available, and not as much Mainstream money as expected. (It should be noted that the pressure to keep Mainstream and Neighborhood Youth Corps *out* of the CEP came as much from the federal staff connected with those programs as it did from the local project sponsors themselves. In fact, it is entirely likely that some of the sponsor pressure was generated by federal field staff.)

The 1968 plans for CEP also included a portion of the state grant funds earmarked for the Human Resource Development (HRD) program of the Employment Service. It seemed reasonable to pool HRD money with other CEP funds, since HRD was exactly the kind of service we were trying to make available through the CEP. However, it is almost impossible to control the use of the trust funds once they are apportioned to the states; Human Resource Development funds never did get into the CEP as planned. Quite the reverse happened; in city after city the CEP's had to purchase HRD services from the local Employment Service. It is estimated that in FY 1969 approximately $15 million in CEP funds went to local Employment Services.

The developments leading up to the congressional veto on the use of Title I–D funds for the CEP program have been discussed. Since the first year, no Special Impact money has been used for any of the CEP's.

Ideally, a Concentrated Employment Program must be able to offer on-the-job training as one of the services needed by the target population. In the first year of operation, all of the CEP's had authority and funds for OJT in their programs, but because of a lack of employer involvement the OJT components were never fully utilized. With the advent of JOBS, it was clear that the two programs could be advantageously linked. The decision was made that wherever there was a CEP in a JOBS city (JOBS was originally limited to the fifty largest cities), JOBS should provide most of the on-the-job training for the CEP, and that, furthermore, CEP should be the prime source of recruitment for JOBS.[1]

On the whole this arrangement has worked well. CEP sponsors, usually Community Action Agencies, are not as effective as an employer organization like the National Alliance of Businessmen in getting on-the-job training commitments from industry. This is not to say that the spin-off of the on-the-job training component of the CEP's to NAB–JOBS has been without problems. In several instances the training opportunities offered by some employers participating in the JOBS program were for such low-status and relatively low-paid jobs that the local CEP which was supposed to provide trainees for JOBS refused to refer its enrollees to those particular JOBS training slots. Other problems have arisen because the CEP is in a limited and sharply defined target area, while JOBS encompasses an entire metropolitan area, and there have not always been adequate transportation arrangements to bring them together. A third difficulty has been in the limited number of on-the-job training slots compared to the number of CEP enrollees for whom OJT would be most appropriate. One CEP has solved this problem by strictly limiting its intake to the number of job or training slots available to it at any one time. Most of the CEP's, however, have tried to maintain an open-door policy, on the theory that some service, no matter how inadequate, is better than none at all—a policy that undoubtedly has led to some of the disenchantment with the CEP.

The decrease in the number of funding sources for the CEP, serious as it has been, has not been as significant as the insistence, and growing success, of HEW in maintaining a sort of apartheid for the institutional portion of the MDTA. In the first round of CEP agreements, the MDTA funds were included in the contract between the sponsor and the Department of Labor. Regular procedures were always followed for MDTA institutional projects, with control over the money split between HEW and the Department of Labor. HEW controls the funds for instructional costs of training. The Department of Labor pays trainee allowances.

It was an essential part of the CEP concept that there be a *single* contract with a *single* sponsor for *all* manpower services needed by disadvantaged residents. "All" manpower services obviously includes skill training. By including the institutional MDTA funds in the contract, the sponsor had the opportunity of purchasing the skill training necessary for effective operation of his program from the local vocational education system, if feasible, or from some other source if vocational education could not do the job. Some state agencies, however, encouraged by the Bureau of Adult and Vocational Training in HEW, interpreted this as unauthorized and illegal use of "their" money. Some officials have even accused the Department of Labor of "stealing" state funds; this despite the fact that HEW took part in the original planning for CEP, and that, furthermore, it was at White House direction that the CEP was initiated.

As a result of the hue and cry raised over this issue, HEW was able to have included in the 1968 MDTA amendments provisions which now make it harder to include institutional MDTA as part of a single CEP contract.[2] HEW is now insisting on separate contracts. This means that the sponsor no longer has the flexibility or the control over funds that he had before. The local vocational education system is now frequently in the driver's seat in the determination of the amount, kind, time, and place for CEP skill training. In addition, if HEW has its way, skill training and other classroom instruction (basic education) that is presently being provided directly by CEP sponsors (where the vocational education system was rot able to satisfy the sponsor's needs) using other than MDTA funds, may have to be channeled through the state vocational education system.

As it now stands, CEP is funded from two sources, the CEP versatile account (Title I–B of the EOA) and the MDTA—but institutional MDTA is usually outside the contract with the sponsor. The other manpower programs like the Neighborhood Youth Corps, Operation Mainstream, and the Work Incentive Program all run separately, even though they draw enrollees from the same target group as the CEP. The result may be that the CEP will become something quite different from what it was at the outset. Instead of a conglomerate of all manpower resources tied together in one program, the CEP will become more limited in scope, directing itself entirely to "employability" and referral services. If that is the case, the CEP will be in direct competition with the Human Resources Development program of the Employment Service. It is not likely that coexistence will be easy, or even worth achieving. It will be ironic indeed if the Concentrated Employment Program, which held such promise for coordinating the local manpower programs and for resolving the costly and debilitating struggle between the Employment Service and the Community Action Agencies, ends up as a means of intensifying that struggle.

## LINKING MANPOWER PROGRAMS

Although there is a continuing struggle for the action—a struggle that may be bitter and even rough—the local operators of manpower programs will probably reach some sort of accommodation, some sort of *ad hoc* arrangement that works. It may not work as well as it should or could, but it will work. This is why any attempt to disrupt that arrangement by the imposition of what is hoped to be a more effective system will very likely run into all kinds of opposition.

In Philadelphia, the Opportunities Industrialization Center (OIC) operates a program of occupational skill training in five or six separate locations in and around North Philadelphia. The vocational education division of the Philadelphia school system operates a large skill center in South Philadelphia, the John F. Kennedy Center for Vocational Education. The OIC does a first-rate job of recruiting the hard-core. Its "feeder" program appears to get at the motivation problem better than most manpower programs. OIC places its enrollees in good jobs, but there is a very high dropout rate from the program. The J.F.K. Center is well equipped, has a dedicated staff, and is capable of training in a variety of skills readily marketable in the Philadelphia area. Its dropout rate is much lower than OIC's, but many of its slots are unfilled. Obviously the two groups ought to make use of each other's capabilities and resources, but they don't. Each is very scornful of the other and believes that there is no benefit to be derived from any sort of cooperation. One man at the OIC says of the J.F.K. Center: "They have nothing we need." And, indeed, the need in Philadelphia is so great that the two groups, independently, can do a job without getting in each other's way—not yet anyway.[3]

In New Bedford, Massachusetts, where there is a tight labor

market and a tremendous need for skilled and semi-skilled production workers, offers another example. The city's vocational education school is filled to capacity and is demonstrably inadequate to the need. Thus the school system did not object when the CEP instituted its own skill center, training its enrollees in a variety of skills. At the present time this arrangement is working. But when the capacity of the school system increases, as scheduled, it seems certain that there will be conflict.[4]

## MANPOWER IN COMMUNITY REHABILITATION PROGRAMS

In addition to the problems of local coordination, there are the even more difficult problems of linking manpower with broad human and economic development community rehabilitation programs. The relationship of the Model Cities program to CEP is a good example. The Demonstration Cities and Metropolitan Development Act was enacted in late 1966, and initial planning got underway in 1967 with the development by HUD of application, review, and approval procedures. In March 1967, the Department of Labor announced the beginning of the Concentrated Employment Program. Obviously the two programs were related, and there was no question but that they should be coordinated.

The Manpower Administration made a policy decision that, to the extent the funds would permit, CEP's would be located in cities that were to become Model Cities. Furthermore, target areas for the two programs were to be compatible, if not exactly the same, and every effort was to be made to establish the CEP as the manpower component of the broader Model Cities program. Unfortunately, the policy has been only partially successful. Although almost 80 percent of the present CEP's are located in cities approved for the Model Cities program, the number of Model Cities far exceeds the number of CEP's, with the result that only 40 percent of the Model Cities have CEP's. Furthermore, even when a CEP was set up in a Model City, and target area boundaries were successfully rationalized, getting the two separate planning groups to work together proved difficult. The scope of the unmet needs and competing local interests have more often than not worked to keep the planners apart. It is rare, indeed, to find a city where the CEP is actually the manpower component of the Model Cities program.

Several other forces have worked against coordination of these two programs. There is a time lag between the beginning of operations in each program. All CEP's have been in operation for from one to two years, and some are now in their third year, while most of the Model Cities have yet to begin operations. By June 1969, only 35 cities had received action grants. As a result, plans and decisions have had to be made on the CEP's without reference to the Model Cities program. Also, the extension of the CEP to additional cities has not kept pace with the growth of the Model Cities programs. In addition, the decision to make the JOBS program nationwide has meant that the priority for limited manpower dollars formerly enjoyed by the Model Cities program has slipped; it now must be shared with JOBS cities. As is so often the case, conflicting priorities and parochial interests have gotten in the way of rational policy.

Duplication of effort and competition between various groups may be tolerated for a time, but there is no question that it is expensive, both in staff and in other resources. And the most serious consequence of the lack of coordination is that without coordination there can be no rationally planned growth or development of national manpower policy.

In the Manpower Administration we tried to get coordination by exerting outside pressure, as in the case of the CEP. We hoped to get it by encouraging cooperation and accommodation of local interests. However, the failure to hold all of the pieces of the CEP together, and the failure to tie the CEP to the Model Cities program underscore the need to try fresh approaches if effective coordination is ever to be achieved.

# 5
## The Federal Structure—
## Organization and Reorganization

The roadblocks that stand in the way of the conscientious federal program administrator are numerous and tricky. His authority is a tenuous thing, drawn from laws that are developed in the crucible of conflict, compromise, and accommodation, or passed on to him like a hand-me-down suit, tailored for another owner in another era. He must fight the Washington bureaucratic battles with at least moderate success. He must master the maze of federal-state-local relations and turn them to his advantage. He must understand the business of resource allocation and how to distribute limited funds. And if the administrator is to be able to deal with all of this and make some headway in achieving the goals of his program, he must also have an efficient and effective organization. Indeed, the success or failure of national manpower policy is predicated on the existence of a strong federal administrative structure to undergird the entire manpower system. For me, the struggle to build such an organization was a continuing one, time consuming, often frustrating, but not without rewards.

My experience with the problems of administrative organization not only serves as a lesson in the politics of government administration but is a basis for my belief that it is possible to make the institutions of government—however barnacle encrusted they may

74

be—respond positively to changing social policies. The process is a slow one. It sometimes contains moments of drama and suspense. It always involves the play of pressure politics. And if the process is to yield results, it requires, above all, perseverance and patience. This is the story of attempts during my tenure as Manpower Administrator to rationalize the federal manpower structure.

When I took office in January 1965, the Manpower Administration existed in name only. It consisted of two strong old-line bureaus, the Bureau of Employment Security and the Bureau of Apprenticeship and Training, and two relatively new and untried offices, an Office of Manpower Automation and Training (OMAT) and an Office of Financial and Management Services (OFMS). The Bureau of Employment Security was the federal fiefdom of the State Employment Security system, with jurisdiction over the Unemployment Insurance and Employment Service systems. The Bureau of Apprenticeship and Training, established to administer the union-supported Fitzgerald Act of 1937 for the promotion and protection of the apprenticeship system, was particularly responsive to the Metal and the Building and Construction Trades Unions. Both bureaus had for some time enjoyed a more or less autonomous existence within the Department of Labor—a common enough position for many of the special interest bureaus that make up the constituent elements of federal departments. OMAT and OFMS had been established in 1963 to implement sections of the Manpower Development and Training Act. Like the two older Manpower Administration bureaus, OMAT had its own regional offices and field staff.

It was clear to me that the creation of a Manpower Administration considerably stronger than the existing loose confederation of independent bureaus was a priority objective. If the new national manpower policy and programs were to work, there had to be an efficient federal organization to provide the direction and assistance on which success depended. Ideally, such an organization should consist of a coordinated national staff and a unified field organization controlled by a single line of authority from headquarters. Operational authority for programs should be decentralized to the regional level to the maximum extent consistent with carrying out the manpower legislation and national policy.

## EARLY PLANS

Although I did not know it whan I accepted the appointment offered to me by Secretary Wirtz, John Donovan, my predecessor as Manpower Administrator, and other top officials in the Department concerned with manpower were also thinking in terms of reorganization. As a result of a 1964 study, a reorganization proposal based on a single line of authority to regional manpower administrators who would have authority for unified administration of all Manpower Administration elements, was circulated within the Department. The directors of the Bureau of Employment Security and the Bureau of Apprenticeship and Training were both opposed to what they believed was a diminution, if not the abolition, of their authority. When details of the plan became known to the state Employment Security agencies and to the AFL-CIO, the opposition solidified. For different reasons, but with equal vehemence, the AFL-CIO and the state Employment Security administrators found a rare occasion to team up against the proposal—the unions because they were afraid the plan would compromise their interest in the apprenticeship program, and the Employment Security administrators because it meant absorption of their "friend in court" into a broader administrative structure. (Until the Bureau of Employment Security came under threat of absorption or abolition, the state agencies were prone to regard it as their natural enemy—an agent for harassment, interfering unnecessarily in purely state affairs. But, as is so often the case, the threat of "outside" intervention drew the Bureau and the state agencies together, and they acted in concert to ward off the new common enemy.)

Although I agreed with the intent of the proposed reorganization plan, I was opposed to its adoption at that time. I knew of the opposition that had developed, but that was not the reason for choosing to wait. I naturally wanted a little time to get a firm grasp on the existing structure before attempting something new.

76

Moreover, I felt that it did not matter what the organizational structure looked like so long as one exerted good strong leadership; with patience and persistence I felt I could resolve problems as they arose and bring the existing organization along to carry out the programs and policies that various situations demanded. Ultimately, I found that this was an overly optimistic view, that persuasion, logical argument, and even firm direction are not sufficient. Finally, the proposed plan would have continued in important administrative positions those individuals who—with congressional backing and a carefully cultivated constituency—stood for the preservation of the status quo and against any change. Under such circumstances no reorganization could hope to succeed.

My concern about putting the proposed reorganization into effect was confirmed during my first appearance as Manpower Administrator before the House Appropriations Committee in March 1965. Representative John Fogarty of Rhode Island, Chairman of the Appropriations Subcommittee on Labor, Health, Education, and Welfare, let me know in no uncertain terms how he felt about *any* reorganization.

Mr. Fogarty: I assume you know the feeling of this committee on the proposed reorganization? If you do not, we will spell it out for you later on. But you have been around here for two days now and I would assume you know the feeling.
Mr. Ruttenberg: Mr. Chairman, may I say a word on the subject?
Mr. Fogarty: You can say anything you want to say.
Mr. Ruttenberg: . . . I would like to have it understood, if I might Mr. Chairman, that I specifically said the very first day that I became the Administrator that I did not think the reorganization should go into effect. . . .
Mr. Fogarty: May I say, good for you.

. . . . . . . . . . . . . . . . . . . . . . . . . . . . . . . . . . . . . . . . . . . . . . . . . . .

Mr. Fogarty: I am not going to belabor the point. As far as I am concerned, my mind is made up on the question of this reorganization of your Department. Mr. Goodwin (the Director of the Bureau of Employment Security) has been here through several Administrations and four or five Secretaries of Labor. The Secretaries of Labor come and go, but Mr. Goodwin stays on. I think Mr. Murphy (the Director of the Bureau of Apprenticeship Training) will stay on regardless of who is Secretary tomorrow or next year, or five years from now.

Mr. Ruttenberg: I think that is unquestionably true.

Mr. Fogarty: The Congress has always supported these two agencies and there is no doubt in my mind as to how the Congress will respond to this proposal. I thought I made it clear yesterday, but I am trying to make it clearer right now. Is that clear?

Mr. Ruttenberg: Mr. Chairman, it was quite clear to me yesterday.

Mr. Fogarty: Let's get on.[1]

## ESTABLISHMENT OF REGIONAL MANPOWER ADMINISTRATORS

For the next year and a half I carried out my responsibilities without resorting to any major organization changes within the Manpower Administration, trying to provide strong leadership and hoping thereby to attract the bureau heads to join the team. During this period the range and scope of the manpower effort increased tremendously. A new bureau was added to the Manpower Administration to handle the Neighborhood Youth Corps program, but like the other bureaus it had its own regional and district offices. By the summer of 1966 it was clear that we could not begin to do an effective job of coordination, particularly at the local level, until we faced up to the problem of overlapping and conflicting federal manpower field structures. The work of the three-man teams served to underline the point.

As a start toward better coordination it was decided to set up Manpower Administration Regional Executive Committees (MAREC) in each of eleven regions.* These committees were to be made up of the regional administrators or directors of each of the constituent bureaus of the Manpower Administration: the Bureau of Employment Security, the Bureau of Apprenticeship

* The Bureau of Employment Security and the Bureau of Apprenticeship Training each had eleven regions. The Neighborhood Youth Corps, following the OEO pattern, had seven. Gradual rationalization of boundaries and reduction in number of regions was a long-standing goal finally achieved in the realignment of late 1967 when we moved to a standard eight-region pattern. On March 27 and May 21, 1969, President Nixon announced a further rationalization of regional boundaries for the Departments of Labor, HEW, HUD, the OEO, and the Small Business Administration, increasing the number for the Manpower Administration to ten.

Training, and the Neighborhood Youth Corps. The committees were to meet at least once a month, with the chairmanship rotating among the three principals. Liaison was established between MAREC and the national office, with information on programs and policies that overlapped bureau interests being channeled from the national office to MAREC. For the first time, the people with operational responsibility for manpower programs in the field were brought together on a regular basis to exchange information, discuss problems of mutual concern, and communicate those joint concerns to Washington in an orderly and systematic fashion. However, without any one person having authority and responsibility in the field as the Manpower Administrator had in Washington, and without staff support or a permanent chairman, or even a regular meeting place, MAREC could not be very effective.

The new programs that crossed bureau lines—first CEP and CAMPS, then the Neighborhood Center Pilot Program and the Model Cities program, and finally the JOBS program—required a degree of coordination that could not be satisfied by the informal kind of operation that characterized MAREC. Moreover, without clear authority for MAREC, coordination remained on a voluntary basis. This was true for the older single-purpose programs as well as for the newer, more comprehensive programs.

In short, I came to realize the hard way that organizational structure was very important. Some people do not respond to leadership and soft appeals for cooperation. They play the hard bureaucratic game of self-preservation. Furthermore, they play it even harder when they have an organization like the Interstate Conference and its concomitant congressional support behind them. Although change can sometimes be brought about by voluntary responsiveness to leadership, I learned that more often leadership must be backed up by clearly defined responsibilities and lines of authority. I realized why there had been an imperative in late 1964 for a reorganization of responsibilities and a single line of authority to a unified field structure. However, the pressures against centralization remained. The necessary structural changes would have to be accomplished gradually. The first step had to be the establishment of regional manpower administrators.

During the fall of 1966, in connection with the preparation of the FY 1968 budget, discussions with the Bureau of the Budget on the need for new positions for regional manpower administrators were initiated. The President's budget each fiscal year includes a request for authority to fill a specific number of positions, or jobs, to administer federal programs, as well as the more publicized request for money to meet federal program objectives. Both the Bureau of the Budget and the Appropriations Committees give as much or more attention to these position requests as to the dollar requests. However, when the President's budget for FY 1968 was presented in January 1967, it included the Manpower Administration request for eight regional representatives, who were to be the new regional manpower administrators.

By the time we went before the House Appropriations Subcommittee in March 1967 to present the FY 1968 budget, Mr. Fogarty had died and Representative Daniel Flood of Pennsylvania was the new chairman. When Secretary Wirtz first explained the need for eight regional representatives at the regular committee hearing, Mr. Flood appeared understanding and sympathetic to the problems we were having with coordination. Furthermore, his interest in economy and efficiency tended to make him willing to let us take whatever administrative steps we believed necessary. Although Representative Flood had no objections to the proposal, it was necessary to get the approval of other members of the committee, particularly the ranking minority members. We also needed to get approval from the key people on the House Ways and Means Committee, which has jurisdiction over the Unemployment Insurance system—a tax matter—and which is, therefore, concerned with any manpower issue that touches on the administration of that system.*

* Administration of the federal-state Employment Security system is financed under the Federal Unemployment Tax Act which imposed a .4 percent payroll tax on employers. The money, collected by the states as agents for the U.S. Treasury and deposited in a trust fund in the U.S. Treasury, finances the administration of the Unemployment Insurance system (UI) and the Employment Service system (ES), both of which were the responsibility of the Bureau of Employment Security.

Representative Wilbur Mills, the chairman of the committee, along with other committee members were wary of any proposal that would affect the control of the state Employment Security agencies over the Unemployment Insurance program. Before they would approve the new positions they wanted to be assured that the Unemployment Insurance system and the management of the trust fund for that system would not be disturbed. The chief issue, therefore, in the months-long negotiations that took place with members of the several committees concerned with manpower affairs in both houses of the Congress was the scope of authority we intended to give to the regional manpower administrators. We had started with the thought that the regional administrators should have line authority over the separate bureau field structures. But the congressional committee members wanted us to limit authority to staff functions and, particularly, to leave untouched the authority of the Bureau of Employment Security over the operation of the state Employment Service and the Unemployment Insurance system.

At one point I thought we had worked out a compromise with the appropriate committees of the Congress, but when that fell through, the round of conversations and negotiations began anew. Finally, agreement was reached with all parties. We were permitted to establish regional administrators, but on the understanding that they would be staff, not line positions, that their duties would be limited to coordination and would not include direct supervision of other bureau field staff, and that each regional administrator would have under his direct supervision only a secretary and perhaps a deputy. It was also understood, however, that the regional manpower administrators would have complete authority for the development and operation of the *new* programs that crossed bureau lines, such as CEP, CAMPS, and Model Cities. They would, of course, assume chairmanship of MAREC. During the fall, the new regional administrators were selected, and by November 1 they were functioning in seven regions.[2]

## THE 1967 REALIGNMENT

Coordination of field operations was not the only urgent organizational problem facing us in the summer and fall of 1967; there was in addition, a tremendous need to improve individual program operations. The new Work Incentive Program, about to be enacted in the Social Security Amendments of 1967, posed a real question as to where and how it should be administered within the Manpower Administration. The On-the-Job training program under the MDTA was in serious trouble. Not only was the program not getting to the disadvantaged target group to the extent anticipated but it was not achieving the goal for the "coupled" OJT program—the linking of classroom training, including basic education, to training on the job. The root of the problems with On-the-Job training seemed to lie more in an unsatisfactory administrative structure than in faulty program design. In addition, the heavy workload entailed in the management of the program was forcing the Bureau of Apprenticeship and Training, which had On-the-Job training responsibility, to give inadequate attention to the promotion and development of the national apprenticeship program—a situation that could not be tolerated for long.

Planning and other staff functions were dispersed throughout the Manpower Administration, with each bureau providing its own staff services. Even contracting was being done in several different places, with no consistency or central control. With the advent of CEP and other comprehensive programs, the Manpower Administration found itself in the ridiculous position of expecting local sponsors to have a broader and more technical knowledge of the various manpower plans than most of its own staff, both in Washington and in the field. It is ironic, but true, that for a period the only Manpower Administration personnel having working knowledge and familiarity with all manpower programs and options were a few journeymen-level contract officers who had worked on the first round of CEP contracts in 1967.

Finally, there were two external, but equally compelling, forces behind the impetus to reorganize. First, the President had directed all federal agencies to review their operations with a view toward further administrative economies; the escalation of the Vietnam War was beginning to be felt, creating inflationary pressures that required government restraints. Second, though there had been for some time a movement within the federal government to rationalize the regional and field organizations of the various federal agencies, the Bureau of the Budget was again actively pressing this point.

Without question, the time was ripe for reorganization. On December 19, 1967, Secretary Wirtz announced a realignment, modifying the distribution of functions and responsibilities within the Manpower Administration.[3] The Bureau of Apprenticeship and Training was relieved of the responsibility for the OJT program so that it could put full time and effort into developing and promoting the apprenticeship program. All manpower program operations except the institutional portion of MDTA were centralized in one bureau, the Bureau of Work-Training Programs, "so as to achieve an integrated work-training program." This meant that the Economic Opportunity Act programs—Neighborhood Youth Corps, New Careers, and Operation Mainstream—as well as the MDTA on-the-job training, and CEP were brought together in one operating bureau. In addition, responsibility for the Work Incentive Program was lodged with the Bureau of Work-Training Programs, not with the Bureau of Employment Security as some of the State Employment Security agencies had expected. However, as Secretary Wirtz made clear in his December 19 memorandum, responsibility for carrying out all Bureau of Work-Training programs at the local level, including WIN, would rest with the state agencies as much as possible. "Many of the state agencies have developed a significantly increased capacity for administration of the work training aspects of the manpower program; and this should be relied on to the fullest practicable and most effective extent. . . . The functions of the BWTP will be carried out to the fullest practicable and effective extent through the system of state employment service offices." The MDTA institutional program, which operated on an entirely different set of procedures involving both the state Employment Security agencies and the vocational education system, was left with the Employment Service. Common regional offices were established for all of the constituent bureaus of the Manpower Administration. Responsibility for planning, policy development, evaluation, research, and experimental and demonstration projects was centralized under an Associate Manpower Administration. Financial and management services, except those relating to the administration of the Unemployment Trust Fund, were centralized under an Assistant Manpower Administrator.

As anticipated, opposition developed immediately from three principal sources: senators and congressmen representing districts where regional offices were scheduled to close; some local unions and employers who were concerned about the shift of the On-the-Job training program; and the Interstate Conference of Employment Security Agencies.

Congressional pressure was relieved by assurances that the level of local Manpower Administration representation would be maintained, if not through regional offices, then through district or local offices. Pressure from the unions and employers was really localized. In fact the AFL-CIO was pleased to have the Bureau of Apprenticeship and Training free to do its traditional work. And local employers soon adjusted to dealing with a different government bureau.

However, the Interstate Conference opposition took a more serious form. In early January the Executive Committee of the Interstate Conference met in New York and voted seven to five to oppose the realignment. Dissatisfaction with our decision to give the WIN program to the Bureau of Work-Training Programs instead of to the Bureau of Employment Security was the chief reason for the opposition. Although it was clearly understood that the state agencies would have operational responsibility at the local level for carrying out the program, the bone of contention was which federal bureau the state agencies would be required to deal with. With the Bureau of Employment Security they obviously felt safe. With the Bureau of Work-Training Programs, made up to a large extent of the new influx of poverty fighters, they were uncomfortable.

Although the Interstate Conference had been able to frustrate proposed reforms before (particularly in regard to improvements in the Unemployment Insurance program), this time the only result of their opposition was a minor flurry of letters and telegrams —which soon subsided—from some members of Congress and other groups representing the Bureau of Employment Security power base. The realignment certainly did nothing to increase our popularity with the Interstate Conference, however.

## THE 1968 REORGANIZATION

Work began immediately to put the new plan into effect, drafting organizational details, shifting personnel, and so on. To make sure that the plan was understood by all concerned, in early January 1968 the Under Secretary of Labor James Reynolds and I, accompanied by the entire top staff of the Manpower Administration, made a tour of the regional offices for a series of meetings with the federal field staff, state Employment Security Administrators and State Apprenticeship Directors.

At the same time we were involved in launching—again with White House support—still another new manpower program. For several months planning had been underway, with both White House and Bureau of the Budget participation, for a program to encourage increased private industry involvement in finding solutions to the problems of hardcore unemployment. The result was the announcement by the President in his Manpower Message to Congress on January 23, 1968, of the formation of the National Alliance of Businessmen and the initiation of the JOBS program. From the beginning, it was planned that the newly established regional manpower administrators would have responsibility in the field for the development and operation of this important program.

Concurrently with the negotiations on the Hill in 1967 over authority for the establishment of regional manpower administrators, the Department of Labor had begun discussions with the

Bureau of the Budget and the Civil Service Commission to make these jobs supergrades.[4] In order to attract and hold the top quality staff the job required, it was clear that the positions must be upgraded. The added responsibility of the JOBS program made the case even stronger. Furthermore, the White House was on our side. The President had stated in his Manpower Message that he was asking Congress for sixteen new supergrade positions for the Manpower Administration. "We must have top administrators now—both here in Washington and in the eight regions across the country in which these manpower programs will operate."[5]

For the President to ask for the positions and for the Labor Department to get them were two different things, however. For months we tried in vain to persuade the Civil Service Commission to give us the supergrades. But even with White House intervention, the Commission stood firm. Chairman John Macy felt that he could not meet our request because he had reached his legislative ceiling and also because he could not take positions away from other agencies to give to us since he did not have from us a strong enough description of the responsibilities of the regional manpower administrators. Without such a description in writing, the Commission was unwilling to order other agencies to give up positions. We could not comply because of the understanding we had reached with the Congress on the issue of regional administrators in the summer of 1967. Exasperating as that stalemate seemed to me at the time, I still believe that the commitment made to the Congress was right. There had to be a first step, and establishment of regional manpower administrators with limited authority was it.

As programs proliferated and manpower became big business— a $2 billion budget in FY 1969—this stalemate on the regional manpower administrators was only one evidence of the increasingly obvious need for a strengthened administrative structure. In March 1968, Secretary Wirtz directed me to take the necessary steps to improve administration of our programs, particularly in the field. The only way to create the administrative machinery capable of properly carrying out the national manpower policy was by a second reorganization which would clear up existing ambiguities and establish clean lines of control and authority throughout the Manpower Administration.

In June 1968, Assistant Secretary Leo Werts, members of my staff, and I met with White House and Bureau of the Budget staff to map out a strategy for such a reorganization. First, it was suggested that the impact of the reorganization would be greater if it were announced by the President, even though there was no question that as an internal departmental matter it could be carried out by the Secretary of Labor on his own authority. I agreed with this proposal. The important decision was made that the announcement of the reorganization would come from the White House. Second, in order not to jeopardize, even slightly, the President's legislative program still under consideration by the Congress, it was decided to wait until after adjournment before announcing the reorganization. Since it was an election year there was reason to think that the Congress would adjourn early, but of course it did not.

I took the responsibility for getting everything in order. My staff began work immediately on drawing up a reorganization plan. To make sure that everything went smoothly, and to forestall the development of effective opposition, we felt it important that there be no premature disclosure or general discussion of the plan. For this reason the planning group was kept purposely small.

The completed plan was not too different from the one I had rejected in 1965 when I first took office. Essentially it unified the separate elements of the Manpower Administration into rational staff and line organizations. A single line of authority was established from the Manpower Administrator to the regional manpower administrators who were to act as the Administrator's counterparts in the field. Full authority would be delegated to them for managing, within established policy guidelines, the manpower programs in their regions. They were to be given strong line control over all federal manpower regional and field units. The Bureau of Work-Training Programs and the United States Employment Service were to be combined into one unified Employment and Training Service. BWTP, USES, and the Bureau of Employment Security were to be abolished as separate entities. The Unemployment Insurance Service was to be elevated within the Manpower Administration, and along with the Bureau of Employment Compensation it was to report to a new Associate Manpower Administrator for Insurance and Compensation.[6] The plan also called for separate offices of Evaluation, Manpower Management Data Systems, and Information, each reporting directly to the Manpower Administrator; and for further centralization of administrative and other staff functions both in the regions and at headquarters. The Bureau of Apprenticeship and Training was to be relocated under the Assistant Secretary for Labor-Management Relations.

During the summer we met repeatedly with White House staff to keep them informed of our progress. We were continually assured of the President's support for the reorganization, and since the plan was consistent with the President's great interest in manpower as earlier expressed in his Manpower Message, there was no reason to doubt the assurances given to us. In one of the White House discussions we were asked to prepare a memorandum setting out the problems we expected to encounter and how we proposed to deal with them. Subsequently, at White House instruction, we proceeded to take the steps outlined and to touch all the bases we had agreed should be covered before congressional adjournment.

Secretary Wirtz and I checked with the key congressional leaders, particularly with those on the appropriations and authorization committees. There were no objections. It was an election year, and given a natural inclination to keep out of the internal administrative affairs of the executive branch, they were not eager to divert attention from other pressing matters.

We were satisfied that prior discussion with the governors was not necessary. We been assured by the White House on this point, and the Bureau of the Budget agreed that the procedures for consultation with the governors called for in a Bureau instruction to federal agencies (Circular A–85) did not apply. Conversations had also been held with the AFL-CIO and with key officials of the National Alliance of Businessmen.

We discussed the plan with the top Manpower Administration

staff, including Robert Goodwin, Administrator of Bureau of Employment Security; Hugh Murphy, Administrator of the Bureau of Apprenticeship and Training; and Mark Battle, Administrator of the Bureau of Work-Training Programs. They were willing to go along with the plan as announced. I also talked to some of the state Employment Security administrators. Finally, plans were made for another series of meetings across the country, very like those held in January 1968 after the announcement of the December 19, 1967, realignment, to explain the reorganization to the field staff of the Manpower Administration and to the state agencies. By late September, all of the decks were cleared. All but one.

As the congressional session dragged on and on throughout the summer and early fall, our hopes for an early adjournment faded and our timetable for the announcement and implementation of the reorganization had to be revised. By the first week in September the timing of the reorganization in relation to the election had become an issue. I felt strongly that the reorganization was not and should not be put into a political context. The creation of a strong streamlined Manpower Administration was too important to the achievement of manpower goals to risk in a political arena. For this reason I felt that the reorganization would have to be undertaken before the election, now less than a month away. It was my belief that if we waited until after the election the reorganization was certain to be given a political interpretation. If the Democrats won, it would be said that we waited in order to keep the Democratic vote in line. If the Democrats lost, the reorganization would be interpreted as the backhanded maneuver of a sore loser. Our decision to announce the plan before the election gave us only three weeks between the final adjournment of Congress on October 14 and the election on November 5, not enough time, as it turned out, to successfully carry out our carefully laid plans.

Immediately after the adjournment Secretary Wirtz and I met at the White House with the Special Assistant to the President, Joseph Califano, and his aides to go over the final arrangements. At that meeting we were shown a memo prepared for the President on the reorganization. There was a place on the bottom of the page where the President could check yes or no. We were again assured that the President would check yes. After this meeting Secretary Wirtz left town to do some campaigning for Hubert Humphrey, the Democratic presidential candidate.

On the assumption that it would only be a day or two at the most before the reorganization was announced by the White House, and with the full knowledge of the White House staff, I called a meeting of all the regional manpower administrators for Saturday morning, October 19, to inform them of the plan and to alert them to their responsibilities in implementing the new organization. During the week I was also discussing new assignments with the headquarters staff and starting the process of putting the proposed plan into effect.

Late in the week I received a call from the Under Secretary, James Reynolds, who was acting Secretary in Mr. Wirtz's absence. Reynolds indicated that there were some second thoughts at the White House about having the reorganization right now. He reported that he had asked for a meeting for Secretary Wirtz with the President and that Mr. Califano had agreed to try to set something up probably for the following Wednesday, though the President had a pretty full schedule. The Under Secretary and I agreed, however, that we had no choice but to go ahead with the Saturday meeting with the regional manpower administrators.

On Saturday, while the regional manpower administrators and the top executive staff of the Manpower Administration were in my office discussing the details of the reorganization plan and their new assignments, I received a call from the Under Secretary who had just concluded another conversation with a White House aide. He reported that President Johnson definitely did not want to proceed with the reorganization, but White House aides still hoped they could arrange a meeting between Secretary Wirtz and the President sometime during the coming week. I instructed the regional manpower administrators and the others at the meeting not to move ahead until they heard from me. At this point, we were only two weeks away from election day. We were fast running out of time.

On Sunday Secretary Wirtz called me at my home. He had just returned from his campaign swing and had been briefed by the Under Secretary on what had happened.

We talked for more than an hour. The Secretary felt that we could not afford to wait for a meeting with the President—a meeting that was still very indefinite. Up to this point the Secretary had received no direct communication from the President about the reorganization; neither had Under Secretary Reynolds, nor, of course, had I. Furthermore, since we had been led to believe all along that the President favored the plan and that we were acting in accordance with his instructions in making preparations for its implementation, we assumed that President Johnson's apparent hesitation in approving the reorganization at this point was a temporary concern, directed not at the substance of the plan but at the time, place, and circumstances surrounding its announcement. The Secretary felt that we had gone too far to turn back and that since this was a purely internal administrative matter over which he had authority, he would go ahead and announce the reorganization on his own. I was aware of some of the problems that such an announcement would create, but I concurred with his analysis of the situation and agreed that we should proceed. On Monday, October 21, the announcement of the reorganization was made by Secretary Wirtz from the Department of Labor. On Tuesday, a mass meeting of all Washington Manpower Administration staff was held and a full explanation presented of what was to happen under the reorganization. The regional administrators were instructed to move ahead with implementing the plan. In addition, preparations were made jointly with the Governors' Conference to send copies of the reorganization to all governors.

Why did we act without the President's consent? I can only speak for myself—but I find in the Secretary's words a better description of my motivation than I could provide. As he wrote in the Fifty-Sixth Annual Report of the Secretary of Labor, January 1969:

There was particular attention in the Department in 1968 to the first obligation of Government, which is self-government. There had been the almost sudden ignition during the first half of the decade, of the national purpose to eliminate inequalities of human opportunity. The Department of Labor had become a full partner for the first time in implementing that purpose. Consequent pressures on and inside the Department had been met for two or three years by administrative improvisation. Now, with the initial impact of new responsibility absorbed, it was time for major basic adjustment in departmental structure and operations. . . . But if the custodians of inertia are in retreat, they are not disbanded. . . . Labor remained by far the smallest among the Cabinet departments. Various bureaus were moved in and out of it, their personnel scattered around in 20 or more buildings in Washington and in a widely divergent pattern of regional offices across the country. The comparative recency of acrimonious controversy about whether some of these bureaus would permit their telephone calls to be handled through the Department switchboard illustrates how much and how long the Department of Labor remained hardly more than a loose-knit confederation of agencies. That attitude and situation began to change in the late 1950's. The change accelerated in the early 1960's. Although there are still significant residues of it there is every reason to conclude that nothing stands today between the Department of Labor and its maturity except its own sloughing off of institutional habits and attitudes traceable in large part to a half century of orphanage—or being an unwanted child—in the family of Federal departments.

The self analysis which proceeded in the Department in 1968 was tougher-minded and more pragmatic than this introduction of it may suggest. It was *not* dominated by sensitivities about the past, or by any regard for institutional status as an end in itself. It proceeded rather from the clearest possible identification of *human* purposes that the Department can best serve.

For six years—eight for the Secretary—we had struggled to put into effect a massive new program to improve the lot of people handicapped in one way or another insofar as employment is concerned, using antiquated machinery that made the job twice as hard as it should have been.

The reorganization was the final step in what had been a long struggle to build an organization capable of carrying out the heavy responsibilities put upon us. I knew, as did Secretary Wirtz, that our reorganization plan was essential to the proper functioning of the manpower programs, and so did the top White House staff;

that it was vital if the programs designed to help those most in need were to become meaningful. We knew that if we could not accomplish the reorganization now, it would be postponed for a long time. We could not in good conscience let this opportunity go. I felt that it was not only our right to go ahead with the plan, but our duty.

President Johnson did not see it the same way. Tuesday night, a day after the announcement, I got still another call from Under Secretary Reynolds; the Secretary was again out of town. Reynolds reported that the President had just called him at home. had severely reprimanded him for announcing the reorganization, and had told him to get Secretary Wirtz to withdraw the announcement. At noon on Wednesday, Secretary Wirtz went to see the President. When he returned about 2:00 P.M., he went directly to his office without talking to anyone. I went to see Under Secretary Reynolds to find out what had happened. Reynolds didn't know. But about 3:00 P.M., while I was there, Reynolds got a call from Mr. Califano, asking him if he would accept the position of Secretary of Labor. The Under Secretary hesitated. Mr. Califano indicated that if Reynolds accepted, the White House would expect him to rescind the reorganization order. Reynolds said he would accept the job but would not rescind the order.

I did not see Secretary Wirtz until later that afternoon. When I did, he told me what had happened at the White House meeting with the President. Mr. Johnson was very angry and let Wirtz know it. He asked the Secretary to rescind the reorganization order. When Wirtz refused, the President demanded that the order be rescinded. Wirtz then returned to his office and decided to comply with the President's demand but to submit his resignation. By the time he had completed his letter of resignation and prepared an order rescinding the reorganization, the working day at the Department of Labor had ended, so it was too late to distribute the order. The Secretary decided to hold it until morning and then have it distributed. I told the Secretary that I could not in good conscience remain if the reorganization order was rescinded and that I would also resign. He suggested that it would be best if he sent his resignation to the White House first; I could send mine in the morning. I agreed and went home to write a letter to the President.

Thursday morning at 7:30 A.M., the Secretary called me to say that he had just had a call from the President, who said he had received the resignation but that before accepting it he wanted a copy of the order rescinding the reorganization. The Secretary was firmly convinced that the President intended to get the reorganization called off and then not to accept the resignation. I concurred with that view. The Secretary stood his ground; acceptance of the resignation became the *quid pro quo* for the rescinding order.

However, the events that were to make it impossible to go ahead with the reorganization, but at the same time preserve the integrity of the Administration, had been set in motion. Wednesday afternoon, a few hours after Secretary Wirtz left the White House, a copy of a telegram to the President from Buford Ellington, Governor of Tennessee, Chairman of the National Governors' Conference and an old friend of the President's, was logged into the Department of Labor. The telegram raised objections to the reorganization on behalf of the Governors' Conference and asked the President to call a halt.[7]

On Thursday, the Secretary received two emissaries from the President. First he was visited by Clark Clifford, then the Secretary of Defense, who was sent by the President to try to talk Wirtz out of his position. Then Warren Christopher, the Deputy Attorney General, came to see him. Mr. Christopher came with instructions from President Johnson to explain to Mr. Wirtz what the powers of the President were in regard to his Cabinet officers. However, Christopher, a long-time friend of the Secretary also wanted to work out a compromise. He suggested that the status quo be maintained, leaving the order in effect but holding up implementation until after the election. The President did not want a big blow-up in his Cabinet just before the election; neither did Secretary Wirtz. The Secretary felt, with the President, that such a blow-up could only hurt Vice President Humphrey's rather slim chance of winning. While he did not feel that he could rescind the order and go back to the organization that existed before, he was willing to postpone putting it into full operation if doing so would prevent the political boat from being rocked. Several drafts of a telegram from Secretary Wirtz to Governor Ellington were prepared before language satisfactory to all parties was finally agreed to. As it was finally sent, the telegram invited the governors to meet with the Secretary on November 8 to discuss their objections to the plan and stated that "we will hold the matter in status quo here and will postpone effectuation of the projected action until such discussion."[8] This left the reorganization order intact but met the governors' request to be consulted before the plan was put into operation.

When the meeting finally took place on November 12, state Employment Administrators acting as representatives of their governors were more in evidence than the governors themselves. It was apparent that the governors had no real objections to the plan at all. In fact, at this meeting Governor Hulett Smith of West Virginia, Chairman of the Manpower subcommittee of the Governors' Conference, said that he hoped the whole issue of the reorganization could be discussed and approved at the next meeting of the Governors' Conference, scheduled for early December in California. That would have made it possible to move ahead with the reorganization. However, it was never discussed at the California meeting and our situation remained unchanged.

The decision was then made *not* to rescind the reorganization order, and *not* to go forward with implementation. This decision to leave matters in a state of uncertainty and confusion was deliberate, even though we knew it would work some hardship on the loyal and hard-working staff of the Manpower Administration. It was made in recognition of the impropriety of a major reorganization just before a change of administration, and in the hope that by continuing the state of uncertainty we would force the incoming Administration to make an immediate decision, a decision we were sure had to be *for* reorganization. As it turned out, we were right.

There is no question at all in my mind about where responsibility for the collapse of the reorganization effort lies. It lies with the President, and with the White House staff. As I reflect on that long and difficult summer, I am now inclined to believe that the President was not informed of our intention to reorganize or made aware of any of our activities. It is my impression that with the President so preoccupied with international and defense affairs the White House staff took his support for granted and did not bother to keep him informed on the almost eight months of discussion that had taken between the White House staff and myself. The President may well have been for the reorganization in the early part of the summer, but as time wore on, the situation changed.

However, we made some mistakes of our own. One was to wait so long to put the plan into effect; it could have been done very easily and smoothly much earlier in the summer. Another was to leave some bases uncovered; we should have consulted with the governors even though we were advised to the contrary. But the biggest mistake—and this was mine—was to involve the White House at all. The reorganization could have been announced and accomplished within the Department of Labor without presidential involvement. The Secretary of Labor certainly had the authority, as do all Cabinet officers, to organize his own department. We should have used it. But on repeated occasions we were told that the reorganization would add to the President's prestige, that it would be an appropriate and lasting contribution to the success of his domestic policy, and that above all, he wanted it to be recognized as *his* reorganization.

The unanswered question is, of course, why did the President take such a strong stand on what was a relatively minor administrative matter, especially at a time when international events were certainly uppermost in his mind. I can only surmise. For twenty-two days, from October 9 to November 1, the President personally managed a series of negotiations on the question of the total bombing halt. Just before the beginning of those negotiations, on September 24, Secretary Wirtz had made a speech in Sacramento to the California Federation of the AFL-CIO, in which he publicly broke with the President on the Vietnam issue.

It may have been that the press reports of this speech contributed to the President's anger with the Secretary, and that the well-known

Johnson temper rose to a boiling point because the President felt that Secretary Wirtz was being "disloyal" in a way he would not tolerate. However, I think it is also likely that the President may have reacted to the way the reorganization was handled; it came with no forewarning at a time when more pressing matters were demanding his total attention, and, furthermore, at a most inappropriate moment vis-à-vis the election.

If we had known the extent to which the White House staff presumed to act for the President in this matter, we would better have foreseen the result of our decision to go ahead without the President's approval. The fact that we misjudged his reaction to such an extent is a comment on the extraordinary pressure and isolation in which Cabinet officials, as well as the second echelon, worked during the Johnson days.

This story needs only one brief postscript. One of the first acts of the new administration was to put into effect, with minor changes, the reorganization we did not achieve. Without in any way detracting from its success, or its great effort to touch all bases and obtain universal support, I believe that it would not have been possible had we not paved the way.

# 6

## A Model for the Organization
## and Delivery of Manpower Programs

Time and time again in the preceding sections we have pointed to the confusion and inefficiency that exist when there are several, often conflicting, legislative mandates, planning bodies, and administrative structures. Most authorities on manpower as it relates to the employment problems of the disadvantaged will agree that the need for better coordination is the predominant issue of the day. Indeed, several legislative proposals to rationalize existing manpower programs and planning and delivery systems are currently under discussion.[1] Without question, we must call a halt to the disorderly proliferation of systems in single areas. However, what is needed is not necessarily a consistent pattern that permits one kind of operator to dominate all of the others, but a pattern that permits federal authority and guidance while at the same time encouraging the necessary flexibility to satisfy local needs and take advantage of local capabilities.

The model proposed here for the organization and delivery of manpower programs, though certainly not perfect, is admittedly somewhat ideal. It does, however, take into account existing manpower institutions and arrangements and works toward a reasonable solution of their problems. Although it would be difficult to achieve, I firmly believe in its eventual practical acceptance and utility.

## CRITERIA FOR EFFECTIVE ORGANIZATION OF MANPOWER PROGRAMS

In building any system, one must begin with the individual who is the target of the manpower efforts, and with what must be done to provide him with a program that meets his needs. Translated into program terms, this means that there must be available in a local community an array of manpower services that make it possible for each individual to take full advantage of those manpower services.[2] The array must be truly comprehensive and must include provision for the usual employment services (help to individuals in finding jobs), services aimed at rehabilitation or preparation for employment, manpower training, work experience leading to employment, and subsidized employment in the public sector. (To assure that all kinds and degrees of individual employment needs can be met and satisfied, both residential training and public employment must be included among the options available to a community. Unfortunately, this is not the case today). In each locality the program must be broad enough to allow tailoring to the needs of individuals and flexible enough to be geared to the specific problems of the community.

In developing a comprehensive manpower system that will achieve this, meet national manpower goals, and provide a viable planning mechanism, as well as effective operational machinery, there are several basic criteria which must be met.

1. The system must allow for strong federal direction. In the attainment of national goals and fulfillment of public policy, the federal executive must be given the authority and develop the capability for effective administration of the total manpower effort. Not only must the federal government determine policy and set standards for performance, it must also enforce conformity through continuous monitoring and review of ongoing programs.

2. Elected officials must be held accountable for both the planning and the operation of manpower programs within their jurisdictions. This is necessary because public accountability can only be assured in the long run through political processes. The

federal government has a responsibility to assure that the programs are administered efficiently and without fraud or misuse of the tax dollar, but it cannot act as the final judge of whether or not the programs are locally acceptable. If the programs are not meeting local needs, and are not acceptable, the local residents ought to be able to exercise control through the ballot box.

3. Giving responsibility to elected officials is not enough, however, to assure equitable treatment of the disadvantaged, since until recently the poor have been effectively disfranchised, and in many localities this is still the case. Therefore, there must also be provision for the participation of the people for whom the programs are intended in their planning and in their supervision. Inclusion of the poor in the administration of the programs has valuable program implications (i.e., the use of neighborhood residents as outreach workers), but unless they are included in the decision-making process in a significant way, participation in administration will amount to nothing.

4. States have legitimate responsibilities, which they must meet, for the social and economic welfare of the people who live within their borders. The states do have considerable authority. They exercise control over a large portion of the manpower and manpower related resources. This authority and these resources must be turned to serve national goals.

5. Manpower planning must be related to other social and economic programs in a community. It must be related to supportive services as well as to national priorities. If the national decision is to continue to give priority to the Model Cities program, manpower must be tied closely to that effort. Similarly, if the proposed welfare reform is adopted and becomes a national top-priority program, manpower planning at every level of government will have to be related to the welfare program.[3]

6. Manpower planning must take into account the availability of employment. Therefore, employers must be included in the planning process from the beginning.

7. Since the impact of manpower falls most directly on workers, labor must also be included in the planning. Policies and programs designed to affect the size, quality, and availability of the

labor force will, by definition, affect the lives of working men and women. They must therefore have a voice in the planning process.

8. Effective planning and administration requires a lead time long enough for the planners and administrators to weigh—it is hoped judiciously—available resources against total needs. This requires at least a two year authorization, and a two year planning cycle instead of the present one year cycle.

9. Ultimately, the success of the system lies in the hands of those who administer it. The quality of personnel depends on a well-developed program of training and recruitment.

10. In our society, an entirely new organizational system usually cannot be successfully installed without considering the strengths and weaknesses of the existing structure. For this reason the establishment of a new system must be a phased operation, gradually moving from where we are to where we want to be.

## The Model

One way to organize the manpower system would be to have the federal government administer all local programs directly or, if not that, to exercise firm control by contracting on a project basis with federally selected sponsors. The other extreme would be to turn over the entire manpower responsibility to the states, through block grants or some form of revenue sharing. The first course is not practical, and the second would leave the cities, particularly the large cities with the most serious poverty problems, at the mercy of the states. The model proposed here strikes a middle course, utilizing the state capability but giving the necessary protection to the cities.

## A. *The Local Planning Board*

1. To the maximum extent possible, each local area should develop a local planning capability under the direction of the mayor or the chief elected executive. The "local area" would, of course, be a political jurisdiction, in order to preserve the principle of political responsibility. Local planning must be on a city-wide basis. This does not preclude concentration of effort in selected

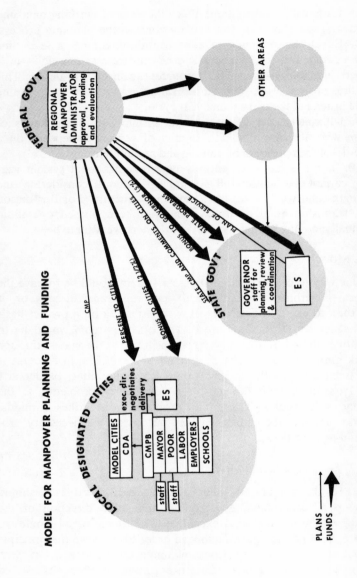

MODEL FOR MANPOWER PLANNING AND FUNDING

target areas, but it does assure coordination with other programs and promotes the best utilization of all community resources.[4]

2. This planning board, called here the Comprehensive Manpower Planning Board (CMPB), would be shaped on the Model Cities concept of control by the chief city executive. In fact, in the Model Cities the Board would be the manpower component of the City Development Agency. The CMPB would consist of the mayor (who would be the chairman), a representative of the poor, of the employers (presumably the National Alliance of Businessmen wherever it is organized), of labor, and the superintendent of schools. The local area manager of the Employment Service might also be included, though since he is a state man he should not be a voting member.

3. Representation of the poor on the planning board and on the staff could be satisfied in one of several ways. One possibility would be to include the Community Action Agency on the planning board as an advocate of the poor. Another would be to establish an advisory citizens' council—either elected or selected by the poor—bringing to the planning board a balancing force against city hall, which is generally perceived as the establishment.

4. The board members would select and hire an executive director who would be responsible to the CMPB.

5. A possible staffing pattern could follow the Model Cities bicameral arrangement of two planning staffs, one hired by city hall and the other by the citizens' council, or a council of the poor. A confrontation is almost certain, but the requirement for agreement between the elected officials and the poor as the price of federal approval would create sufficient pressure on the two staffs to work out their differences. If the program is to be responsive to the needs of the poor, as it must, then there is no alternative but to force accommodation of the two groups. It must be recognized, however, that the federal government should stand ready to move into potential stalemates and to assist in the resolution of differences. A word of caution: unfortunately, difficult situations, resolved once, don't always stay resolved and may require continuing federal intervention. A less satisfactory but alternative staffing pattern would be to have a single planning staff, with the requirement that a certain number of poor people be hired to work on the staff.

6. While the CMPB was developing its manpower plan, the local Employment Service area manager would be developing his plan of service. This plan, prepared annually for each local office and for the state as a whole, provides the basis for funding of the state Employment Service agency. In the plan, the agency must describe what services it expects to provide, where and how they will be provided, and to whom. The local area manager would be required to fit his plan of service to the CMPB. If he did not, it would not be approved at the federal level and no funds would be provided to the Employment Service in that city for any purpose, including service to groups other than the disadvantaged. In the unlikely event that the Employment Service would fail to accommodate to the CMPB, the CMPB would be free to shop elsewhere for the provision of manpower services.

7. Just as the Employment Service is *required* to fit its plan of service to the CMPB, the CMPB should start its planning with the full understanding that the Employment Service is *expected* to become the chief local operational arm of national manpower policy.

8. After the CMPB plan and the Employment Service plan of service have been negotiated and agreed to, both would be submitted as one package to:

—the City Development Agency in Model Cities, where they would become the manpower component of the Model Cities program.

—the Regional Manpower Administrator who would have final approval of all plans; and

—the governor, to give him an opportunity to coordinate his program for the balance of the state with the city plans, as well as to coordinate the manpower program with related education, health, vocational rehabilitation, welfare, economic development, and so on. It is at this point, too, that the governor has the chance to force coordination of the State Employment Service with the city programs.

9. The planning process that is being carried out under the aegis of the mayors in the designated cities would be duplicated, insofar as possible, for the balance of the state under the aegis of

the governor. His concern would be for the rural areas without independent planning capacity and for localities other than the specific cities previously designated by the federal government. For the purposes of this model, those cities are Model Cities plus the JOBS cities.

10. Both the designated cities and the states would require funding to develop adequate planning capability. Money for this purpose should be provided by the federal government.

11. All plans—both the state and the designated city plans—would go the Regional Manpower Administrator who would have final approval authority. In submitting the state plan to the administrator, the governor would have an opportunity to add his comments on the city plans. However, negotiation on designated city plans would be carried out directly by regional manpower administrators with the mayors, while negotiations on the "balance of the state" plans would be carried out with the governors.

12. Obviously the system would have to permit the governors the right of appeal over the regional manpower administrators to the Secretary of Labor. However, every effort should be made to insure the decentralization created by this system through strengthening the regional manpower administrators. Upgrading the position itself and giving them sufficient, well-trained staff would provide greater leverage for direct, authoritative negotiations with the governors.

## B. *Program Administration*

### 1. *Allocation of resources*

The system proposed here assumes that the federal government will make a preliminary allocation of resources to the planning groups so that they will not be planning in a vacuum but can balance local needs against the realities of what can reasonably be expected. Furthermore, it is assumed that the basic allocation of resources will conform to the national manpower goals. For the purpose of this model it is assumed that the principal national manpower focus will remain on the poverty problem and on the related city problem. If the focus were to shift to, for example, the development of policies and programs to meet what promises to become a dangerous shortage of technical and scientific personnel in the area of environmental control, new legislation would have to be enacted and new systems devised for effective administration of the programs.* Similarly, if a drastic change in the national economic situation—that is, a severe economic depression—made it necessary to mount a large-scale public employment program, taking precedence over the present emphasis on structural unemployment, additional legislation, appropriations, and delivery systems would be required.

Assuming that all of the existing manpower program dollars were brought together—specifically, the funds now provided under the MDTA, the Economic Opportunity Act, the Work Incentive Program, those portions of the Vocational Education Act funds earmarked for training the disadvantaged in poverty areas and the handicapped, and the Vocational Rehabilitation Act—an initial division of those funds could be made on the following basis:

30 percent off the top as a federal discretionary fund; for national contracts, contingency use, and national programs not specifically targeted for the disadvantaged, such as upgrading programs in skill shortage areas;

62.5 percent to be distributed among the states for use in programs for the disadvantaged, including the handicapped;

5 percent to be distributed as bonus payments to states that demonstrate an ability to coordinate manpower programs and meet national priorities;

2.5 percent to be distributed as bonus payments to city mayors who demonstrate ability to develop effective plan-

* There is a continuing and legitimate question as to whether the Department of Labor and the Manpower Administration should have responsibility for the development and administration of manpower policy and programs to meet the full range of national manpower requirements, particularly for assuring an adequate supply of technical, professional, and scientific personnel where the problem is one of advanced education and long-term preparation rather than the malfunctioning of the labor market. For several years now, in recurring discussions concerning the functional organization of the federal executive branch, proposals have been made for the establishment of a department of education and manpower. This suggestion has been put forth in the hope of resolving many of the conflicts that now exist between those who view manpower primarily as an educational problem and those who view it as an employment problem.

ning and operating capabilities and to coordinate manpower programs with other social and economic programs.

Two important budget items, presently included in the total
manpower budget, have purposely been omitted from this discussion. First, the funds that are not specifically program dollars—
have been left out—funds that are used to pay for such activities
as research, evaluation, and experimental and demonstration
projects. These activities do not lend themselves readily to any pre-
set distribution formulas or patterns.

Second, although a part of the present Job Corps residential
training in urban areas has been included—the so-called minicenters
which are properly a part of the array of services that a local community should make available to its disadvantaged, and which in this
model would be a part of the total planning dollars made available
to local planning bodies—the balance of the Job Corps has been
left out. There will continue to be a need for a nationally run Job
Corps to provide training opportunities for those youths whose
dispersion, isolation, or special needs make the establishment of
local training facilities impractical and uneconomic. In addition,
there is a need for a national conservation program—a conservation program to which the national Job Corps can contribute. For
these reasons, the funds for a federally operated Job Corps should
not be considered as part of the general distribution pattern (nor
should they be subject to the same evaluative criteria as other
manpower dollars).

The important point in planning the allocation of resources is
that the federal government should make the basic decisions on
national manpower goals and priorities, but once those decisions
are made and the guidelines set, the federal government should re-
serve for national control and approval only that proportion of the
funds necessary to meet emergency, contingency, and special
needs, or special-purpose funds which are so small that an even
distribution among the states would negate the program goal.

The 62.5 percent of the total program resources which are to be
used for local programs for the disadvantaged and handicapped
would be allotted among the states on the basis of a formula that

puts primary emphasis on the total population distribution but that takes into consideration poverty, unemployment, and geographic differences. Other factors could be considered, such as local effort, public assistance load, youth unemployment, underemployment, levels of education, and draft rejection rates. Table 2 provides a comparison of selected apportionment factors among several test states. To avoid severe program disruptions that could occur as a result of replacing the existing distribution formulas with this one, adjustments would have to be permitted during the first year or two under the new system.

In addition, the federal government would have determined which cities it wants to give priority to. As has been mentioned, this model assumes the priority cities to be the Model Cities plus the JOBS cities. In view of a decision to make JOBS a nationwide program, the cities to be included might be the Model Cities plus all other cities over 200,000 population. If national priorities demanded, it is possible that one might want to add designated "growth centers."

Within each state a certain proportion of the manpower resources allotted for that state would be reserved for use in the designated cities, and the proportion reserved would again be determined on the basis of the formula as applied to the cities.

The Regional Manpower Administrator would have the responsibility of notifying the CMPB in each of the designated cities of the amount of resources available to that city. He would also notify the governor of each state of the total amount coming into his state, and of the amount reserved for the designated cities. The balance then would become available to the governor for planning purposes. He would encourage the same local planning procedure that obtains in the designated cities, but the decisions as to which parts of the state, and which disadvantaged persons—outside of the designated cities—should get manpower dollars would be his decision. The mix of programs would also be his decision.

The mayors would have the same discretion on how the money should be spent—as long as it is used for the disadvantaged. The checks at both levels would be that all of the money must be used for programs for the disadvantaged in accordance with federal

Table 2. Comparison of apportionment factors used in selected distribution formulas.

*(in percentages)*

| Test States | MDTA Apportion-ment FY 1969[a] | NYC Apportion-ment FY 1969[b] | Poverty Population[c] | Weighted Poverty Population[d] | Total Population[e] |
|---|---|---|---|---|---|
| California | 14.63 | 8.9 | 5.5 | 6.4 | 9.5 |
| Kentucky | 1.55 | 2.2 | 2.9 | 2.3 | 1.7 |
| Michigan | 5.17 | 3.5 | 2.9 | 3.2 | 4.3 |
| Mississippi | .96 | 2.0 | 2.9 | 2.6 | 1.2 |
| New York | 10.24 | 8.5 | 6.1 | 8.5 | 9.3 |
| Ohio | 4.39 | 4.0 | 3.8 | 4.1 | 5.3 |
| Pennsylvania | 4.96 | 5.1 | 5.0 | 6.7 | 6.0 |
| Tennessee | 1.75 | 2.5 | 3.5 | 2.9 | 2.0 |
| Texas | 3.35 | 5.9 | 7.6 | 6.4 | 5.5 |
| Utah | .57 | .5 | .3 | .4 | .52 |

[a] Apportionment based on labor force, unemployment, lack of appropriate full-time employment, insured unemployed, average weekly compensation benefits.

[b] Apportionment based on population, unemployment, family income.

[c] 1965 population estimates.

[d] Based on geographical equivalence index developed by Harold W. Watts, Director of the Institute for Research on Poverty, University of Wisconsin. The index takes data from the 1960–61 Survey of Consumer Finances and develops the relative income levels at which the same proportion of income is spent on food and on a larger bundle of "necessities" for each region and community size tested.

guidelines, and the approval of the plans would rest with the Regional Manpower Administrator.

If the governors have done a good job of putting together a manpower plan for the state, if they have been able to make the Employment Service the instrument for implementation of the national manpower program goals, and have involved other state agencies in securing supportive services, they would have available to them the 5 percent of the total funds that were reserved as bonus payments to the states. The decision regarding qualification for the bonus would rest with the Regional Manpower Administrator.

Similarly, if the mayors succeed in bringing together the disparate manpower interests in the city and putting them together into a workable plan which is also part of a broader scheme for social change and economic development, then like the governors, they would get a bonus payment. Two and one-half percent of the total manpower funds would be distributed among the qualifying cities—again with the Regional Manpower Administrator making the final decision on eligibility.

2. *Funding.* Funding of approved manpower programs for the disadvantaged would remain with the regional manpower administrators. In the case of the cities, the administrators would continue to contract directly with the prime sponsor for that city. Since most of the manpower programs do not require state matching, as do many other social programs, the need for a pass-through procedure involving the state government is diminished. (Under present legislation both Vocational Education and Vocational Rehabilitation do require state grants, which in turn are distributed locally in accordance with an approved state plan. While less desirable and more cumbersome than direct contracting, the pass-through could be maintained for these programs.) The programs that are a part of the governor's plan would also be funded directly by the Regional Manpower Administrator in accordance with the approved plan, except it is recognized that there would be some programs administered directly from the governor's office. This would occur in those places where there was no independent planning or operating capability.

Decisions on national special-purpose projects funded from the federal discretionary fund would be made at the national level. Decisions on projects funded as part of other-than-poverty manpower programs (e.g., training in skill shortage occupations) could be made by the regional manpower administrators on the basis of national guidelines and regional allocations.

3. *Sponsorship and Program Operations.* Sound administration requires the separation of planning and operations. It also requires a central point for executive control and management. The concept of the prime sponsor as the focal point for this executive function is a good one and should be maintained.

A parallel is found in the city manager system, where the city council is the planner, allocator of resources, and overseer; the city departments are the operators. The city manager, like the prime sponsor, is in the middle, acting as the agent of the council and as the director of the operators.

In the model, the prime sponsor becomes the fulcrum between the planning and oversight responsibility of the CMPB, on the one hand, and the operations—the actual training, placing, counseling, and so forth—on the other. The sponsor is the agent of the planning and oversight group, but he is also the manager responsible for seeing that things get done.

In order to bring the manpower programs and the Model Cities Program closer together, the prime sponsor for the manpower programs in a Model City should be the City Development Agency, or its manpower component. This could be a Human Resources Agency where one has been established. In the non-Model Cities, the sponsor would again have to be an agency of the city, responsible to the CMPB. Similarly, for manpower programs operated directly by the states, sponsorship would be with a Human Resources Agency, where there was one, or with some other designated agency responsible to the governor and his state planning board.

The operations would then follow one of the two patterns. The preferable pattern would be the assignment of full responsibility for program operations to the local Employment Service. The Employment Service could then either provide all of the services itself, or subcontract components to other local agencies as necessary or appropriate. A second pattern would have the prime sponsor assume the subcontracting responsibility, parcelling out operational components of the total manpower program in conformance with the CMPB approved plan. As a general proposition, the Employment Service should be given as much operational authority as it is capable of handling efficiently and responsively, but it should be recognized that there will be some services better provided by other local agencies. In effect, there would be created a CEP for every major city and Model City, but the "C" would stand for comprehensive instead of concentrated. (It could be both, if that was desired.)

Since institutional training would be a part of the comprehensive manpower plan, the vocational education system would be among the subcontractors in each community. Just as some preference would be given to the Employment Service by forcing a tie-in of its plan of service to the CMPB, preference would be given to the vocational education system by giving it preference in bidding for the institutional training component of the comprehensive plan. Furthermore, the governor would have a better opportunity than before to coordinate his vocational system with the manpower program, since he would be included in the planning process.

LEGISLATION

The proposed model would meet the test of the criteria postulated earlier. It would encourage the development of the comprehensive and coordinated system of manpower assistance in local communities which makes it possible for individuals to get the kind of help that each needs. Now, however, consideration must be given to the legislation necessary to bring this about.

Comprehensive manpower legislation would, I believe, include these basic elements:

1. It would firmly fix in one place responsibility for the development and implementation of national manpower policy.
2. It would authorize a federal-state system of Employment Service offices which could become the chief instrument of national manpower policy.
3. It would provide for the complete range of manpower services and program elements, including outreach and recruitment, rehabilitation and employability service, job development, placement, follow-up, occupational and skill training, on-the-job training, residential training, mobility assistance, career development, and work experience. The legislation should be broad enough to permit shifts in the manpower mix in accordance with national and local needs.
4. It would authorize a program of subsidized employment in the public sector. For some communities, for some groups of people, at some times, public employment is the only

possible solution to manpower problems. The legislation must recognize this fact and be sufficiently elastic to permit establishment of public employment projects as local economic conditions demand and to meet the special needs of particular groups excluded from employment in the private sector.

5. Although the primary emphasis would be on provision of services to the disadvantaged, it would include provision for upgrading the skills of the labor force, both to improve the supply of labor in shortage occupations and to provide additional entry-level jobs for the disadvantaged. It would also include provision for assistance to the technologically unemployed.

6. It would provide a federally operated residential training program for youth—particularly rural youth—who could not be economically provided with adequate or useful employment assistance in their own communities.

7. It would provide for a manpower planning and delivery system that maximized local responsibility but utilized state authority and resources. It would avoid a static structure that inhibited adaptation to different local situations.

8. It would lodge responsibility with the federal administration for monitoring and reviewing ongoing programs, as well as authority to withhold funds from programs and projects that did not meet federally established standards of performance. The *quid pro quo* for decentralization of planning and operations to the states and localities must be their acceptance of federal monitoring and evaluation.

9. It would authorize a continuing program of staff training and recruitment to assure the constant supply of qualified personnel necessary for good administration of manpower programs at all levels.

10. It would provide for a national manpower information network to improve the efficiency of the labor market.

11. It would allow for a national program of manpower evaluation and research, including experimental and demonstration projects.

12. It would include provision for a shift in national manpower policy and program mix in response to national economic fluctuations. For example, the formula for the allocation of resources between the disadvantaged and other manpower needs should not be irrevocably fixed; it should be subject to change as conditions warrant. However, a severe economic depression would undoubtedly set off a new round of legislative activity. It is unrealistic and unwise to expect a single piece of legislation, however comprehensive, to deal adequately with every conceivable contingency.

A comprehensive manpower law which met these specifications would at the minimum embrace the present Manpower Development and Training Act, Titles I and V of the Economic Opportunity Act, the 1967 Amendments to the Social Security Act which established the Work Incentive program for welfare recipients, the 1968 Amendments to the Vocational Education Act which direct Vocational Education funds to the disadvantaged and the handicapped, the Wagner-Peyser Act, and the Vocational Rehabilitation Act. The ongoing programs which would be brought under such a single legislative authority include:

—all MDTA programs: institutional, on-the-job, part-time and other, experimental and demonstration programs, programs carried out jointly with the Economic Development Administration, programs for inmates of correctional institutions, manpower research, and programs carried out by States under the new Title V authority;

—all Title I EOA programs: Neighborhood Youth Corps, in-school, out-of-school, and summer, Job Corps, New Careers, Operation Mainstream, and Special Impact, and the residual authority for the Title V Work Experience program;

—the Work Incentive program;

—the 15 percent of the Vocational Education program that is directed to the disadvantaged, and the 10 percent directed to the handicapped;

—JOBS;

—CEP;

—the recently announced Public Service Career program;

—the Vocational Rehabilitation program;
—the entire Employment Service program, including, but not limited to, the Human Resources Development program. Unemployment Insurance would be excluded.

The college work-study program for the disadvantaged and the high school cooperative education program might also be included. Left out, at least for the present, would be the balance of Vocational Education.

Every attempt should be made to maintain as flexible a funding arrangement as possible. To that end, categorical earmarking of appropriations should be eliminated, but careful accounting procedures should be established to permit congressional identification with favored programs, as well as a continuing and responsive adjustment of national policy to changing economic conditions. Recognizing that Congress is unlikely to accept a single block appropriation for the entire national manpower program, a maximum five-way break is suggested:

1. a separate appropriation for the federal-state Employment Service, preferably from general revenue funds;
2. a percentage from the top of all other funds, to be used as a federal discretionary fund for special purpose and other national programs (in the model this is set at 30 percent);
3. an appropriation for programs directed at the school-to-work problem: the NYC in-school and summer programs, a part of the Job Corps, a part of the NYC out-of-school program, and, if they are included, the work-study and the cooperative education programs;
4. a single appropriation for all other programs for the disadvantaged and handicapped, to provide the complete range of program components, *including public employment*;
5. a separate appropriation for JOBS. This could be lumped with the disadvantaged appropriation, but the existence of a separate account may be the price of continuing employer support and participation in the program.

Why these separations, not more or less? Any separation must be somewhat arbitrary, but these have some rational base.

The Employment Service is separated first because of the uncertainty as to the source of its funding—general revenue or trust funds. But, more important, it is separated to give the federal-state Employment Service system one last chance to become the working arm of national manpower policy. For that reason, this proposal deliberately stops short of federalization of the Employment Service.

The 30 percent reservation of funds to the federal government builds into the legislation the opportunity for a flexible response to changing economic conditions, as well as the ability to meet contingency needs and to carry out national projects that do not lend themselves to state or local administration. Projects aimed at other-than-poverty groups would be expected to be funded from this 30 percent. The fund could also be used, as necessary, to supplement local programs of public employment or to alleviate severe local economic dislocations.

The three-way split of the funds for the disadvantaged may be open to criticism. But it would seem that the school-to-work issue is so markedly different from the issues of employment of the nonschool-age population that separate appropriations are justified. The primary goal of the school-to-work program is to keep young men and women in school so that they can be prepared for employment. The goal of other manpower programs is to get people into jobs, not school.

The JOBS program is suggested as a separate appropriation not because of program differences but because it would seem to be the politic and practical course.

## WHAT ARE THE WEAKNESSES OF THIS MODEL?

Although the word "model" suggests perfection, this model makes no such claim. There are weaknesses, some of which are readily apparent and deserve mention here.

First, the proposed system obviously would give to the state governors more control than they now have over manpower programs. To a certain extent this transfer of authority has to be at the cost of federal control. Furthermore, the model would not give to all governors equally. Some—particularly the governors of rural states—would get considerably more power and authority than they now have, while the governors of the large industrial states would not benefit proportionally. But as checks against misdirection or misuse of the national manpower resources, the system reserves to the federal Regional Manpower Administrator both the final approval of plans and the funding authority. He, of course, will continue to exercise a monitoring function to enforce national standards. Another check is the reservation to the federal government of the basic decisions on the initial allocation of resources, both in terms of the groups of people to be served and of the specific localities to receive priority treatment.

A second weakness is the elimination of the federal HEW–Department of Labor review teams for MDTA institutional training. Granting that they may have become superfluous in large measure, their existence has served as a brake on irrelevant and inefficient training programs. The proposed system would substitute monitoring by regional manpower administrators, a substitution that might not be entirely satisfactory to HEW.

By leaving the decisions on manpower mix to the local planning boards, some capability of responding to changing national conditions is sacrificed. Although there are provisions for adjustments and corrections over time, time may be an important factor in economic policy developments, especially if and as economists master the art of fine tuning.

Present on-the-job training contractors, Neighborhood Youth Corps sponsors, and other program contractors who now deal directly with the federal government and have established working relationships with federal manpower staff both in the field and in Washington will be forced to deal with mayors, CMPBs, or other sponsoring agencies. This is a situation which they undoubtedly won't like, at least for a while.

Organizing the entire system around political jurisdictions, particularly large central cities, ignores the economic concept of the labor market area and penalizes the cities and towns surrounding the central cities. But as long as the economic and social blight of the central cities remains our number one domestic problem, this concentration is justified. Furthermore, it is the central cities that are starved for resources to meet their problems. Suburban or outer-ring cities are generally enjoying an increasing tax base which puts them in a better position to help themselves.

One other question deserves mention. What is the role of the CAAs in this system? Where do they fit in?

First let it be said that there is no doubt at all that the CAAs have performed an invaluable service in focusing public attention on the needs of the poor and in providing all kinds of necessary services which otherwise would have not been provided. The CAAs have had three chief roles: as advocates for the poor, organizing neighborhoods and interceding for the poor with city hall or other government authority; as planners of community programs to combat or alleviate poverty; and as operators of poverty programs, directly or by delegation.

These three functions are interrelated and interdependent, and it is difficult to define where one leaves off and the other begins. In fact, in terms of CAA operations it would be very hard to order the end to one function without affecting the others.

But new developments today make the future of the CAAs unclear. First, the Green Amendment has tempered the advocacy function.

Clearly, the amendment does violence to the original CAA concept. Yet, at least two things may be said in behalf of the change. First, in the long run, it is probably desirable for the CAA's to draw closer to local governments. Second, the CAA role as a lobbyist for social change, while undoubtedly impaired, is nonetheless not precluded under the newer arrangement.[5]

Only one-third of the board are representatives of the poor, and by linking the CAAs to the mayors, the role of the CAA as an interceder becomes somewhat hazy.

Second, the Model Cities program has complicated the planning role of the CAA. When under the Model Cities system the City Development Agency, a creature of the mayor, becomes the central planner, what is left for the CAA?

Finally, although many CAAs have operated effective programs and won the respect and confidence of local leaders, the public attention given to those programs that have been inefficiently and even fraudulently operated has made it difficult for the federal government to encourage expansion of CAA activities and responsibilities. The shortage of technical and administrative expertise may not have been the CAAs fault, but the fact is that this lack of know-how, combined with chronic underfunding, has made it impossible for the CAAs to achieve the high goals originally expected of them. Indeed, a study prepared for the Office of Economic Opportunity by Brandeis University concluded that in only one-third of the CAAs studied were there changes in the policies and programs of other community organizations as a result of CAA activity.[6]

In developing this model we have tried to keep in mind the social revolution facing America, centered at present in the cities. It is a revolution that could reach crisis proportions at any moment. The principles for the organization of manpower spelled out at the beginning of this chapter are predicated on an understanding, insofar as we are able, of what must be done to turn that revolution into constructive social change.

It is the *poor* who must be involved, not the CAAs.

It is the *elected* officials who must take responsibility for promoting change—officials who can be voted out if they fail.

It will take the *best* managerial and technical skills available to administer and operate good manpower programs, skills that can be found and further developed in existing agencies.

It is the *whole* city, not just a target area, that must be concerned with the problems of the poor. All of the resources of the city, the state, and the federal government must be brought together to make any lasting change in the lives of the individuals who desperately need help now.

We have not tried to solve all of the problems of urban organization. We have limited ourselves only to manpower. The future of the CAAs has to be a different question; it is not the central issue in manpower.

# Notes

## CHAPTER 1

[1] Robert S. McNamara, *The Essence of Security: Reflections in Office* (New York: Harper and Row, 1968), p. 107.

[2] U.S. Congress, *Economic Opportunity Act of 1964*, Public Law 88–452, 88th Cong., 2d sess., 1964, sec. 2.

[3] *Ibid.*, sec. 502.

[4] "The entire territory of the United States has been classified by the Bureau of the Budget as (a) metropolitan, or 'inside SMSA's,' and (b) nonmetropolitan, or 'outside SMSA's.' A SMSA [Standard Metropolitan Statistical Area] is a county or group of contiguous counties (except for New England) which contains at least one central city of 50,000 inhabitants or more or 'twin cities' with a combined population of at least 50,000." (U.S. Bureau of the Census, *Statistical Abstract of the United States: 1968* [Washington: U.S. Government Printing Office, 1968], p. 2).

[5] Interviews with state and local officials involved in CAMPS in Massachusetts, Michigan, New Hampshire, and Pennsylvania; with Regional-Federal Manpower Administration officials; and with the U.S. Department of Labor CAMPS evaluation team, April–June, 1969.

## CHAPTER 2

[1] For a complete history of the MDTA, see Garth L. Mangum, *MDTA: Foundation of Federal Manpower Policy* (Baltimore: Johns Hopkins Press, 1968). Additional information on passage of the MDTA can be found in James L. Sundquist, *Politics and Policy: The Eisenhower, Kennedy and Johnson Years* (Washington, D.C.: Brookings Institution, 1968), pp. 83–97.

120

² U.S. Department of Labor, *Manpower Report of the President*, January, 1969, p. 44. (Cited hereafter as *Manpower Report of the President.*) Also see U.S. Department of Labor, *Statistics on Manpower: A Supplement to the Manpower Report*, March, 1969, p. 6. (Cited hereafter as *Statistics on Manpower*, 1969.) Unemployment rates for early 1969 can be found in, U.S. Bureau of Labor Statistics, *Employment and Earnings*, XVI, No. 1 (July, 1969), p. 51.

³ Data on total labor force and teenage unemployment in 1963 derived from *Statistics on Manpower*, 1969, pp. 12–13. Teenagers include youth ages sixteen through nineteen.

⁴ Data on educational status of the unemployed derived from, U.S. Bureau of Labor Statistics, *Educational Attainment of Workers, March 1962*, Special Labor Force Report No. 30, prepared by Denis F. Johnston (Washington: U.S. Government Printing Office, 1963), p. 507. Characteristics of trainees in MDTA projects started in 1963 can be found in *Manpower Report of the President*, 1963, p. 253.

⁵ James L. Sundquist, *Politics and Policy: the Eisenhower*, pp. 83–97.

⁶ In 1963, 3 percent of the trainees were in OJT, and 1.5 percent of the program dollars. By 1969, half of the trainees were in OJT, and about 30 percent of the program money. (*Manpower Report of the President*, p. 238.) The FY 1970 manpower plan calls for a further increase in OJT, primarily through JOBS, so that OJT will outstrip the institutional part of the program in both money and trainees. (Proposed Budget Levels for Fiscal Year 1970, in the files of the U.S. Department of Labor, Manpower Administration.)

⁷ In FY 1965, $183 million was appropriated for the Job Corps, $132 million for the Neighborhood Youth Corps, and $85 million for Head Start. This totaled $400 million for children and youth as compared to $.8 billion—the total budget allocation in FY 1965 for OEO. (U.S. Office of Economic Opportunity, *Management Summary of Anti-Poverty Programs*, February, 1966.)

⁸ "Unearmarked funds" refers to that part of the Community Action Program appropriation which is available to local community action agencies to spend on locally conceived and initiated projects, as distinct from CAP national interest programs such as Head Start, Comprehensive Health Centers, Legal Services, Upward Bound, and Family Planning.

⁹ In the first year the program authorized by the Nelson Amendment had no recognized popular name. It was identified by such projects as Green Thumb and Foster Grandparents, which were developed to implement the purpose of the amendment. In FY 1967, when the program was delegated to the Department of Labor, it was named Operation Mainstream.

¹⁰ Evidence of Senator Nelson's concern for conservation is found in an excellent keynote address he made before the annual meeting of the National Wildlife Federation in Washington, D.C., in March, 1965. (See U.S., *Congressional Record*, 89th Cong., 1st sess., 1965, CXI, Part 5, 6212.)

11 On March 1, 1966, Representative Scheuer introduced H.R. 13159, *To Provide Opportunities for Unemployed and Low Income Persons in Subprofessional Service Careers.* (See U.S., *Congressional Record,* 89th Cong., 2d sess., 1966, CXII, Part 4, 4527.)

12 One section of the House report was specifically titled, "Public Service Employment Training Programs," and the House referred to the Operation Mainstream and New Careers programs as a single program, the Nelson-Scheuer program. Regarding concentration, the House report says the following: "If it is to succeed as a meaningful demonstration, the funds must not be scattered piecemeal into every State and county of the United States, but must, instead, be expended in substantial amounts in the few communities where the highest concentration of chronically unemployed persons are, and where training and employing sizable numbers of such persons in subprofessional capacities can be expected to have the greatest impact upon poverty." (U.S. Congress, House Committee on Education and Labor, *Economic Opportunity Amendments of 1966,* 89th Cong., 2d sess., 1966, H. Rept 1568 to accompany H.R. 15111, p. 10.)

13 "Establishing the President's Committee on Manpower," *Federal Register,* XXIX, no. 76 (April 17, 1964), 5271.

14 Report of the President's Committee on Manpower on the Coordination of Manpower Programs at the Local Level, 1966 (in the files of the U.S. Department of Labor, Manpower Administration).

15 "Office of Economic Opportunity, Secretary of Labor, Delegation of Authorities," *Federal Register,* XXXIII, no. 198 (March 10, 1967), 15139.

16 Named for Representative Edith Green (D-Ore.). This was an amendment to Title II of the Economic Opportunity Act and was designed to bring local Community Action Agencies closer to elected local governments.

17 U.S. Congress, House, Special Subcommittee of the Committee on Education and Labor, *Hearings, Poverty Program,* 89th Cong., 2d sess., 1966.

18 Toward the end of the fiscal year, under certain conditions, money that has been obligated but unspent can be "recaptured" by the government from the project sponsors.

19 U.S. Congress, House, Committee on Education and Labor, *Economic Opportunity Amendments of 1967,* 90th Cong., 1st sess., 1967, H. Rept. 866 to accompany S. 2388, pp. 18–19.

20 *Economic Opportunity Amendments of 1967,* Public Law 90–222, secs. 121–22. Section 123 (a) permits the exclusion of in-school projects as well as JOBS from the CWTP requirements for funding through a prime sponsor.

21 Credit for the development of the CWTP concept and the staff work on this legislative proposal goes to Howard W. Hallmen, director of a special study, "Examination of the War on Poverty," prepared for the Senate Subcommittee on Employment, Manpower and Poverty, of the Committee on Labor and Public Welfare, 90th Cong., 1st sess., 1967.

[22] *The War on Poverty*, A Congressional Presentation, March 17, 1964, pp. 52–57.

[23] *Ibid.*, p. 54.

[24] *Ibid.*, p. 67–68.

CHAPTER 3

[1] U.S., Interagency Cooperative Issuance, *Manpower Coordinating Committee*, Structure and Operation, no. 1, March 3, 1967.

[2] Daniel P. Moynihan, "The Need for a National Urban Policy," address before the Annual Honors Convocation of Syracuse University, May 8, 1969.

[3] U.S. Congress, *Economic Opportunity Amendments of 1967*, Public Law 90–222, secs. 121–22.

[4] U.S. Congress, House, Committee on Education and Labor, *Economic Opportunity Amendments of 1967*, 90th Cong., 1st sess., 1967, H. Rept. 866 to accompany S. 2388, p. 16.

[5] It was my belief, which I stated repeatedly to the ICESA, that the State Employment Service agencies could not hope to be given the responsibility for carrying out the new programs aimed at the urban poor until they showed some willingness to understand urban problems and to work with the elected city officials in solving those problems. As a first step toward more responsive Employment Service participation in solving urban problems of today, the Urban Affairs Committee of the ICESA was created at a meeting of the Interstate Conference in New Orleans in 1967.

[6] Now Manpower Administrator, U.S. Department of Labor, Manpower Administration.

[7] U.S. Department of Labor, *Implementation of Title I-B* of the *Economic Opportunity Act Amendments of 1967*, Manpower Administration Order No. 12–68, October, 1968.

[8] When JOBS was initiated, it was limited to the 50 largest cities. In May 1969 the program was extended to 125 cities, and in November 1969 it was made a nationwide program. However, planning for FY 1970 was done on the basis of 125 cities.

CHAPTER 4

[1] "The primary source [of employee-trainees] will be the Concentrated Employment program (CEP). . . ." (See U.S. Department of Labor, Manpower Administration, *Request for Proposal, MA3–1968*, March 15, 1968, p. 3.)

[2] U.S. Congress, *Manpower Development and Training Act of 1962, as Amended*, Public Law 90–636, 90th Cong., 2d sess., 1968, secs. 204(c) and 231(b).

[3] Interview with personnel at the J.F.K. Center and the OIC, May 26, 1969.

[4] Interview with Mayor Edward Harrington, New Bedford, Massachusetts, June 18, 1969.

## CHAPTER 5

[1] U.S. Congress, House, Subcommittee of the Committee on Appropriations, Hearings, *Appropriations for Department of Labor for 1966*, 89th Cong., 1st sess., 1965, pp. 363–65.

[2] As stated earlier, the Manpower Administration were moving to the same regional pattern as OEO, thus setting up seven instead of eleven regions. An eighth region to cover New England was split away from the original Northeast region and established separately a few months later.

[3] Memorandum from Willard Wirtz, Secretary of Labor, December 19, 1967.

[4] Under the Civil Service system, the regular schedule of grade positions stops at 15. Grades 16, 17, and 18 are called supergrades and are subject to special procedures and regulations. As with the national debt, there is a ceiling—fixed by Congress—on the total number of supergrades. The allocation of these positions among federal agencies is strictly controlled by the Civil Service Commission.

[5] *Manpower Message of the President, January 23, 1968*.

[6] BEC provides workmen's compensation benefits to injured employees under the following principal acts: the Federal Employees Compensation Act; the Longshoremen's and Harbor Workers' Compensation Act; and the District of Columbia Workmen's Compensation Act. The Bureau handles claims and in the case of federal workers makes payments and arranges medical and rehabilitation services. Before this reorganization the Bureau had not been a part of the Manpower Administration.

[7] The telegram, dated October 23, 1968, read:

THE PRESIDENT
THE WHITE HOUSE
I HAVE JUST LEARNED OF THE RULING, HANDED DOWN OCTOBER 22 BY THE U.S. LABOR DEPARTMENT AFFECTING THE EMPLOYMENT SECURITY AND WORKERS' TRAINING PROGRAMS. WE FIND THE ACTION BOTH SURPRISING AND DETRIMENTAL. FURTHERMORE, WE UNDERSTOOD FROM YOUR LETTER OF NOV. 11, 1966 AND THE BUREAU OF BUDGET CIRCULAR A-85 THAT ACTION SUCH AS THIS WOULD NOT BE TAKEN WITHOUT PRIOR CONSULTATION WITH THE NATION'S GOVERNORS OR THEIR REPRESENTATIVES. THE NATIONAL GOVERNORS' CONFERENCE IS ON RECORD AS OPPOSING THIS ACTION AND, AS CHAIRMAN OF THE CONFERENCE I RESPECTFULLY URGE YOU TO IMMEDIATELY RESCIND THE DEPARTMENT OF LABOR'S ACTION.
BUFORD ELLINGTON GOVERNOR OF TENNESSEE AND CHAIRMAN
NATIONAL GOVERNORS CONFERENCE.

[8] This telegram, dated October 25, 1968, read:

HONORABLE BUFORD ELLINGTON
GOVERNOR OF TENNESSEE
NASHVILLE, TENNESSEE
THE PRESIDENT HAS ASKED ME TO REPLY TO YOUR TELEGRAM OF OCTOBER 23 REGARDING THE LABOR DEPARTMENT'S PROJECTED ADMINISTRATIVE ACTION REALIGNING PROGRAM RESPONSIBILITIES IN THE MANPOWER ADMINISTRATION. THE PRESIDENT WANTS TO INSURE THE FULLEST CONSULTATION WITH THE

NATION'S GOVERNORS ON THE IMPACT OF THESE CHANGES ON FEDERALLY-SUPPORTED PROGRAMS AT THE STATE LEVEL (AS ELABORATED IN THE PRESIDENT'S NOV. 11, 1966 AND THE BUREAU OF THE BUDGET JUNE 28, 1967 MEMORANDA TO FEDERAL AGENCY HEADS). ACCORDINGLY, I AM CONTACTING YOU TO ARRANGE TO MEET WITH YOU, A COMMITTEE OF GOVERNORS, OR ANY OTHER REPRESENTATIVE GROUP TO DISCUSS THIS MATTER. WE WILL HOLD THE MATTER IN STATUS QUO HERE AND WILL POSTPONE EFFECTUATION OF THE PROJECTED ACTION PENDING SUCH DISCUSSION. I WILL HOLD NOVEMBER 8 AVAILABLE FOR DISCUSSION, AND WILL OF COURSE CONSIDER AN ALTERNATIVE DATE IF NOVEMBER 8 IS INCONVENIENT FOR YOU OR YOUR COLLEAGUES.

WILLARD WIRTZ

## CHAPTER 6

[1] By August 1969, three major manpower bills had been introduced in the 91st Congress. Representative William A. Steiger (R-Wisc.) introduced *The Comprehensive Manpower Act of 1969*, H.R. 10908. Along with 104 co-sponsors, Representative James G. O'Hara (D-Mich.) introduced *The Manpower Act*, H.R. 11620. The Nixon Administration's bill, *The Manpower Training Act of 1969*, H.R. 13472, was introduced by Representative William H. Ayres (R-Ohio).

[2] As the term is used in connection with manpower training programs, "supportive services" generally refer to the range of work-related remedial assistance—over and above skill training and direct employment assistance—that disadvantaged persons need to solve their employment problems. For example, remedial or basic education, health care, adequate day care for the children of working parents, family counseling, and transportation to the job are among those services classified as supportive. Legal services, consumer protection, and family planning may also be included.

[3] For the text of President's Nixon's Message on Welfare Reform, see U.S., *Congressional Record*, 91st Cong., 1st sess., 1969, CXV, 7239.

[4] The term "target area" has been used in connection with many of the new social and economic development programs of the 1960s to describe the intended concentration of resources in selected areas of poverty or economic depression. In the Model Cities program the concept of co-ordinated planning and operations was originally limited to specific geographically defined areas within a city. However, an early policy of the Nixon Administration extended Model Cities planning to include resources of the whole city, though operations under the program may continue to be limited to specific target areas. (See the *New York Times*, April 29, 1969, p. 1.) Similarly, the Concentrated Employment Program was limited to geographically defined target areas within a city, or to specified counties in a rural area. The question of whether the CEP should be city-wide has not yet been resolved. However, there should be no question but that wherever possible target areas of related federal programs should be coterminous, or at least compatible.

[5] Sar A. Levitan, *The Great Society's Poor Law: A New Approach to Poverty* (Baltimore: The Johns Hopkins Press, 1969), p. 66.

6 "Within this study about one-third of the CAA's have a pattern of target area participation which results in no significant impact on decisions within the CAA or on other communtiy service organizations; in about one-third of the CAA's target area participation does influence some decisions within the CAA . . . but there is little impact on other organizations; and in the remaining third there is a regular and continuing influence on decisions within the CAA . . . and there have been changes in the policies and programs of other community service organizations as a result of target pressure." (Final Report Prepared for the Office of Economic Opportunity, "Community Representation in Community Action Programs," mimeographed [Florence Heller School for Advanced Studies in Social Welfare, Brandeis University, March 1969], p. 46.)